# First German Reader for Beginners

Lisa Katharina May

# First German Reader for Beginners

## Bilingual for Speakers of English

## A1 A2

First German Reader for Beginners

by Lisa Katharina May

**Audio tracks www.lppbooks.com/German/FirstGermanReader_audio/**

Homepage www.audiolego.com

5th edition

Graphics: Audiolego Design

Images: Audiolego Studio

# Inhaltsverzeichnis

Table of contents

A1 Level Course

## How to control the playing speed

The book is equipped with the audio tracks. The address of the home page of the book on the Internet, where audio files are available for listening and downloading, is listed at the beginning of the book on the bibliographic description page before the copyright notice.
We recommend using free **VLC media player** to control the playing speed. You can control the playing speed by decreasing or increasing the speed value on the button of the VLC media player's interface.
**Android users:** After installing VLC media player, click an audio track at the top of a chapter or on the home page of the book if you read a paper book. When prompted choose "Open with VLC". If you experience difficulties opening audio tracks with VLC, change default app for music player. Go to Settings→Apps, choose VLC and click "Open by default" or "Set default".
**Kindle Fire users:** After installing VLC media player, click an audio track at the top of a chapter or on the home page of the book if you read a paper book. Complete action using →VLC.
**iOS users:** After installing VLC media player, copy the link to an audio track at the top of a chapter or on the home page of the book if you read a paper book. Paste it into Downloads section of VLC media player. After the download is complete, go to All Files section and start the downloaded audio track.
**Windows users:** After installing VLC media player, right-click an audio track at the top of a chapter or on the home page of the book if you read a paper book. Choose "Open with→VLC media player".
**MacOS users:** After installing VLC media player, right-click an audio track at the top of a chapter or on the home page of the book if you read a paper book, then download it. Right-click the downloaded audio track and choose "Get info". Then in the "Open with" section choose VLC media player. You can enable "Change all" to apply this change to all audio tracks.

## Das deutsche Alphabet

*The German alphabet*

| Buchstabe<br>Letter | Handschrift<br>Handwriting | Aussprache<br>Pronunciation | Beispiele<br>Examples |
|---|---|---|---|
| A a | A a | ah | Apfel (apple) |
| Ä ä | Ä ä | ay | Äpfel (apples) |
| B b | B b | bay | Buch (book) |
| C c | C c | say | Café |
| D d | D d | day | Doch (however) |
| E e | E e | ay | Rede (speach) |
| F f | F f | eff | Fahren (go, drive) |
| G g | G g | gay | Gast (guest) |
| H h | H h | haa | Hoch (high) |
| I i | I i | eeh | Lippe (lip) |
| J j | J j | yot | Ja (yes) |
| K k | K k | kah | Kuss (kiss, *n*) |
| L l | L l | ell | Leben (live) |
| M m | M m | emm | Mutter (mother) |

| | | | |
|---|---|---|---|
| N n | N n | enn | Nord (north) |
| O o | O o | oh | Ort (place, *n*) |
| Ö ö | Ö ö | oeh | Öl (oil) |
| P p | P p | pay | Preis (price) |
| Q q | Q q | koo | Quadrat (square) |
| R r | R r | err | Rose (rose) |
| S s | S s | ess | Sofa (sofa) |
| ß | ß | ess-zett (s-z ligature) | Straße (street), *lower case only, replaces "ss" in some words.* |
| T t | T t | tay | Tag (day) |
| U u | U u | ueh | unter (below) |
| Ü ü | Ü ü | uyuh | über (over, about) |
| V v | V v | fow | vier (four) |
| W w | W w | vay | Woche (week) |
| X x | X x | ixx | Xylofon |
| Y y | Y y | oop-see-lohn | Typ (type) |
| Z z | Z z | zett | zu (to) |

## Diphthongs

| Diphthong<br>Double Vowels | Aussprache<br>Pronunciation | Beispiele / Examples |
|---|---|---|
| ai / ei | eye | Ein (one), Mai (May) |
| au | ow | auch (also) |
| eu / äu | oy | Häuser (houses), neu (new) |
| ie | eeh | Sie (you), nie (never) |

## Grouped Consonants

| Buchstabe<br>Consonant | Aussprache<br>Pronunciation | Beispiele / Examples |
|---|---|---|
| ck | k | Glük (happyness) |
| ch | kh | Auch (too), sounds like "sh" or like "kh" |
| pf | pf | Pfeil (arrow) |
| ph | f | Alphabet (alphabet) |
| qu | kv | Quark (curd) |
| sch | sh | Schule (school) |
| sp / st | shp / sht | Sprechen (speak), Straße (street) at the beginning of a stem only, otherwise sp/st |
| th | t | Theater (theatre), never pronounced like the English th |

# 1

## Mike hat einen Hund

*Mike has a dog*

 A

### Vokabeln

*Words*

1. auch - too
2. das Auge - eye
3. die Augen - eyes
4. das Bett - bed
5. die Betten - beds
6. blau - blue
7. das Buch - book
8. dieser, diese, dieses - this;
9. dieses Buch - this book
10. diese (Pl.) - these, those
11. ein - one
12. er - he
13. das Fahrrad - bike
14. das Fenster - window
15. die Fenster - windows
16. groß - big

17. grün - green
18. haben - to have
19. er/sie/es hat - he/she/it has;
20. Er hat ein Buch. - He has a book.
21. das Hotel - hotel
22. die Hotels - hotels
23. der Hund - dog
24. ich - I
25. jener, jene, jenes - that
26. die Katze - cat
27. klein - little
28. der Laden - shop
29. die Läden - shops
30. mein, meine, mein - my
31. die Nase - nose
32. neu - new
33. nicht - not
34. das Notizbuch - notebook
35. die Notizbücher - notebooks
36. der Park - park
37. die Parks - parks
38. schön - nice
39. schwarz - black
40. sein, seine - his;
    sein Bett - his bed
41. sie - they
42. der Stern - star
43. der Stift - pen
44. die Stifte - pens
45. die Straße - street
46. die Straßen - streets
47. der Student - student
48. die Studenten - students
49. der Text - text
50. der Tisch - table
51. die Tische - tables
52. der Traum - dream
53. und - and
54. viel - many, much
55. vier - four
56. das Wort, die Vokabel - word
57. die Wörter, die Vokabeln - words
58. das Zimmer - room
59. die Zimmer - rooms

 B

**Mike hat einen Hund**

1.Dieser Student hat ein Buch. 2.Er hat auch einen Stift.

3.Bremerhaven hat viele Straßen und Parks. 4.Diese Straße hat neue Hotels und Läden. 5.Dieses Hotel hat vier Sterne. 6.Dieses Hotel hat viele schöne, große Zimmer.

***Mike has a dog***

*1.This student has a book. 2.He has a pen too.*

*3.Bremerhaven has many streets and parks. 4.This street has new hotels and shops. 5.This hotel has four stars. 6.This hotel has many nice big rooms.*

7.Jenes Zimmer hat viele Fenster. 8.Und diese Zimmer haben nicht viele Fenster. 9.Diese Zimmer haben vier Betten. 10.Und diese Zimmer haben ein Bett. 11.Jenes Zimmer hat nicht viele Tische. 12.Und diese Zimmer haben viele große Tische.

*7.That room has many windows. 8.And these rooms do not have many windows. 9.These rooms have four beds. 10.And those rooms have one bed. 11.That room does not have many tables. 12.And those rooms have many big tables.*

13.In dieser Straße sind keine Hotels. 14.Dieser große Laden hat viele Fenster.

*13.This street does not have hotels. 14.That big shop has many windows.*

15.Diese Studenten haben Notizbücher. 16.Sie haben auch Stifte. 17.Mike hat ein kleines schwarzes Notizbuch. 18.Alexander hat vier neue grüne Notizbücher.

*15.These students have notebooks. 16.They have pens too. 17.Mike has one little black notebook. 18.Alexander has four new green notebooks.*

19.Dieser Student hat ein Fahrrad. 20.Er hat ein neues blaues Fahrrad. 21.Stefan hat auch ein Fahrrad. 22.Er hat ein schönes schwarzes Fahrrad.

*19.This student has a bike. 20.He has a new blue bike. 21.Stefan has a bike too. 22.He has a nice black bike.*

23.Alexander hat einen Traum. 24.Ich habe auch einen Traum. 25.Ich habe keinen Hund. 26.Ich habe eine Katze. 27.Meine Katze hat schöne grüne Augen. 28.Mike hat keine Katze. 29.Er hat einen Hund. 30.Sein Hund hat eine kleine schwarze Nase.

*23.Alexander has a dream. 24.I have a dream too. 25.I do not have a dog. 26.I have a cat. 27.My cat has nice green eyes. 28.Mike does not have a cat. 29.He has a dog. 30.His dog has a little black nose.*

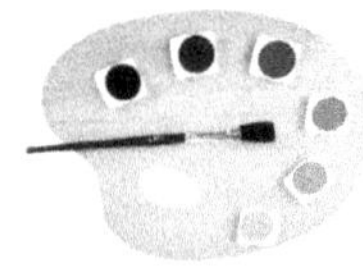

# 2

## Sie wohnen in Bremerhaven (Deutschland)

*They live in Bremerhaven (Germany)*

## A

### Vokabeln

*Words*

1. Amerikaner - American
2. aus - from
3. aus den USA - from the USA
4. der Bruder - brother
5. der Deutsche, die Deutsche - German
6. Deutschland - Germany
7. du - you
8. groß - big
9. hungrig - hungry
   Ich habe Hunger. - I am hungry.
10. in - in
11. jetzt, zurzeit, gerade - now
12. kaufen - to buy
13. leben, wohnen - to live
14. die Mutter - mother
15. das Sandwich - sandwich

16. die Schweiz - Switzerland
17. Schweizer - Swiss
18. die Schwester - sister
19. sie - she
20. die Stadt - city

21. der Supermarkt - supermarket
22. wir - we
23. zwei - two

## B

### Sie wohnen in Bremerhaven

1.Bremerhaven ist eine große Stadt.
2.Bremerhaven ist in Deutschland.

3.Das ist Mike. 4.Mike ist Student. 5.Er ist zurzeit in Bremerhaven. 6.Mike kommt aus den USA. 7.Er ist Amerikaner. 8.Mike hat eine Mutter, einen Vater, einen Bruder und eine Schwester. 9.Sie leben in den USA.

10.Das ist Alexander. 11.Alexander ist auch Student. 12.Er kommt aus der Schweiz. 13.Er ist Schweizer. 14.Alexander hat eine Mutter, einen Vater und zwei Schwestern. 15.Sie leben in der Schweiz.

16.Mike und Alexander sind gerade im Supermarkt. 17.Sie haben Hunger. 18.Sie kaufen Sandwiches.

19.Das ist Linda. 20.Linda ist Deutsche. 21.Linda wohnt auch in Bremerhaven. 22.Sie ist kein Student.

23.Ich bin Student. 24.Ich komme aus den USA. 25.Ich bin zurzeit in Bremerhaven. 26.Ich habe keinen Hunger.

27.Du bist Student. 28.Du bist Schweizer. 29.Du bist zurzeit nicht in der Schweiz. 30.Du bist in Deutschland.

31.Wir sind Studenten. 32.Wir sind zurzeit in Deutschland.

33.Dies ist ein Fahrrad. 34.Das Fahrrad ist blau.

### *They live in Bremerhaven*

*1.Bremerhaven is a big city.*
*2.Bremerhaven is in Germany.*

*3.This is Mike. 4.Mike is a student. 5.He is in Bremerhaven now. 6.Mike is from USA. 7.He is American. 8.Mike has a mother, a father, a brother and a sister. 9.They live in USA.*

*10.This is Alexander. 11.Alexander is a student too. 12.He is from Switzerland. 13.He is Swiss. 14.Alexander has a mother, a father and two sisters. 15.They live in Switzerland.*

*16.Mike and Alexander are in a supermarket now. 17.They are hungry. 18.They buy sandwiches.*

*19.This is Linda. 20.Linda is German. 21.Linda lives in Bremerhaven too. 22.She is not a student.*

*23.I am a student. 24.I am from the USA. 25.I am in Bremerhaven now. 26.I am not hungry.*

*27.You are a student. 28.You are Swiss. 29.You are not in Switzerland now. 30.You are in Germany.*

*31.We are students. 32.We are in Germany now.*

*33.This is a bike. 34.The bike is blue. 35.The*

35.Das Fahrrad ist nicht neu.

*bike is not new.*

36.Dies ist ein Hund. 37.Der Hund ist schwarz. 38.Der Hund ist nicht groß.

*36.This is a dog. 37.The dog is black. 38.The dog is not big.*

39.Dies sind Läden. 40.Die Läden sind nicht groß. 41.Sie sind klein. 42.Dieser Laden hat viele Fenster. 43.Jene Läden haben nicht viele Fenster.

*39.These are shops. 40.The shops are not big. 41.They are little. 42.That shop has many windows. 43.Those shops do not have many windows.*

44.Die Katze ist im Zimmer. 45.Diese Katzen sind nicht im Zimmer.

*44.That cat is in the room. 45.Those cats are not in the room.*

# 3

## Sind sie Deutsche?

*Are they Germans?*

## A

### Vokabeln

*Words*

1. alle - all
2. am, beim - at
3. auf - on
4. das Café - café
5. der CD-Spieler - CD player
6. du/ihr - you
7. es - it
8. die Frau - woman
9. das Haus - house
10. ja - yes
11. der Junge - boy
12. ihr Buch - her book
13. die Karte - map
14. der Mann - man

15. nein - no
16. spanisch - Spanish
17. das Tier - animal
18. unser - our
19. wie - how
20. wo - where

## B

**Sind sie Deutsche?**

1

– Ich bin ein Junge. Ich bin im Zimmer.

– Bist du Deutscher?

– Nein, ich bin nicht Deutscher. Ich bin Amerikaner.

– Bist du Student?

– Ja, ich bin Student.

2

– Das ist eine Frau. Die Frau ist auch im Zimmer.

– Ist sie Amerikanerin?

– Nein, sie ist nicht Amerikanerin. Sie ist Deutsche.

– Ist sie Studentin?

– Nein, sie ist nicht Studentin.

3

– Das ist ein Mann. Er sitzt am Tisch.

– Ist er Deutscher?

– Ja, er ist Deutscher.

4

– Das sind Studenten. Sie sind im Park.

– Sind sie alle Deutsche?

– Nein, sie sind nicht alle Deutsche. Sie kommen aus Deutschland, den USA und der Schweiz.

***Are they Germans?***

*1*

*– I am a boy. I am in the room.*

*– Are you German?*

*– No, I am not. I am American.*

*– Are you a student?*

*– Yes, I am. I am a student.*

*2*

*– This is a woman. The woman is in the room too.*

*– Is she American?*

*– No, she is not. She is German.*

*– Is she a student?*

*– No, she is not. She is not a student.*

*3*

*– This is a man. He is at the table.*

*– Is he German?*

*– Yes, he is. He is German.*

*4*

*– These are students. They are in the park.*

*– Are they all Germans?*

*– No, they are not. They are from Germany, USA and Switzerland.*

5

– Das ist ein Tisch. Er ist groß.

– Ist er neu?

– Ja, er ist neu.

*5*

*– This is a table. It is big.*

*– Is it new?*

*– Yes, it is. It is new.*

6

– Das ist eine Katze. Sie ist im Zimmer.

– Ist sie schwarz?

– Ja, das ist sie. Sie ist schwarz und schön.

*6*

*– This is a cat. It is in the room.*

*– Is it black?*

*– Yes, it is. It is black and nice.*

7

– Das sind Fahrräder. Sie stehen beim Haus.

– Sind sie schwarz?

– Ja, sie sind schwarz.

*7*

*– These are bikes. They are at the house.*

*– Are they black?*

*– Yes, they are. They are black.*

8

– Hast du ein Notizbuch?

– Ja.

– Wie viele Notizbücher hast du?

– Ich habe zwei Notizbücher.

*8*

*– Do you have a notebook?*

*– Yes, I have.*

*– How many notebooks do you have?*

*– I have two notebooks.*

9

– Hat er einen Stift?

– Ja.

– Wie viele Stifte hat er?

– Er hat einen Stift.

*9*

*– Does he have a pen?*

*– Yes, he does.*

*– How many pens does he have?*

*– He has one pen.*

10

– Hat sie ein Fahrrad?

– Ja.

– Ist ihr Fahrrad blau?

– Nein, es ist nicht blau. Es ist grün.

*10*

*– Does she have a bike?*

*– Yes, she does.*

*– Is her bike blue?*

*– No, it is not. Her bike is not blue. It is green.*

11

– Hast du ein spanisches Buch?

– Nein, ich habe kein spanisches Buch. Ich habe keine Bücher.

*11*

*– Do you have a Spanish book?*

*– No, I do not. I do not have a Spanish book. I have no books.*

12

– Hat sie eine Katze?

– Nein, sie hat keine Katze. Sie hat kein Tier.

13

– Habt ihr einen CD-Spieler?

– Nein, wir haben keinen CD-Spieler.

14

– Wo ist unsere Karte?

– Unsere Karte ist im Zimmer.

– Liegt sie auf dem Tisch?

– Ja, sie liegt auf dem Tisch.

15

– Wo sind die Jungs?

– Sie sind im Café.

– Wo sind die Fahrräder?

– Sie stehen vor dem Café.

– Wo ist Alexander?

– Er ist auch im Café.

*12*

*– Does she have a cat?*

*– No, she does not. She does not have a cat. She has no animal.*

*13*

*– Do you have a CD player?*

*– No, we do not. We do not have a CD player.*

*14*

*– Where is our map?*

*– Our map is in the room.*

*– Is it on the table?*

*– Yes, it is.*

*15*

*– Where are the boys?*

*– They are in the café.*

*– Where are the bikes?*

*– They are at the café.*

*– Where is Alexander?*

*– He is in the café too.*

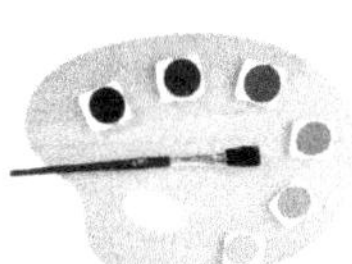

# 4

## Können Sie mir bitte helfen?

*Can you help, please?*

## A

### Vokabeln

*Words*

1. aber - but
2. die Adresse - address
3. die Bank - bank

   Ich gehe zur Bank. - I go to the bank.
4. bitte - please
5. danken - to thank;

   danke - thank you, thanks
6. dürfen, können - may

   nicht dürfen - must not
7. für - for
8. die Hilfe - help; helfen - to help
9. gehen - go
10. können - can

    Ich kann lesen. - I can read.

11. legen - to place
12. lernen - to learn
13. lesen - to read
14. müssen - must

    Ich muss gehen. - I must go.

15. nehmen - to take
16. schreiben - to write
17. setzen - to sit
18. spielen - to play
19. sprechen - to speak

## B

**Können Sie mir bitte helfen?**

1

– Können Sie mir bitte helfen?

– Ja, das kann ich.

– Ich kann die Adresse nicht auf Deutsch schreiben. Können Sie sie für mich schreiben?

– Ja, das kann ich.

– Danke.

2

– Kannst du Tennis spielen?

– Nein. Aber ich kann es lernen. Kannst du mir dabei helfen?

– Ja, ich kann dir helfen, Tennis spielen zu lernen.

– Danke.

3

– Sprichst du Deutsch?

– Ich kann Deutsch sprechen und lesen, aber nicht schreiben.

– Sprichst du Englisch?

– Ich kann Englisch sprechen, lesen und schreiben.

***Can you help, please?***

*1*

*– Can you help me, please?*

*– Yes, I can.*

*– I cannot write the address in German. Can you write it for me?*

*– Yes, I can.*

*– Thank you.*

*2*

*– Can you play tennis?*

*– No, I cannot. But I can learn. Can you help me to learn?*

*– Yes, I can. I can help you to learn to play tennis.*

*– Thank you.*

*3*

*– Can you speak German?*

*– I can speak and read German but I cannot write.*

*– Can you speak English?*

*– I can speak, read and write English.*

4

– Kann Linda auch Englisch?

– Nein, sie kann kein Englisch. Sie ist Deutsche.

5

– Sprechen sie Deutsch?

– Ja, ein bisschen. Sie sind Studenten und lernen Deutsch.

– Dieser Junge spricht kein Deutsch.

6

– Wo sind sie?

– Sie spielen gerade Tennis.

– Können wir auch spielen?

– Ja, das können wir.

7

– Wo ist Mike?

– Er ist vielleicht im Café.

8

– Setzen Sie sich an diesen Tisch, bitte.

– Danke. Kann ich meine Bücher auf diesen Tisch legen.

– Ja.

– Darf Alexander sich an seinen Tisch setzen?

– Ja, das darf er.

9

– Darf ich mich auf ihr Bett setzen?

– Nein, das darfst du nicht.

– Darf Linda seinen CD-Spieler nehmen?

– Nein, sie darf seinen CD-Spieler nicht nehmen.

– Dürfen sie ihre Karte nehmen?

– Nein, das dürfen sie nicht.

4

*– Can Linda speak English too?*

*– No, she cannot. She is German.*

5

*– Can they speak German?*

*– Yes, they can a little. They are students and they learn German.*

*– This boy cannot speak German.*

6

*– Where are they?*

*– They play tennis now.*

*– May we play too?*

*– Yes, we may.*

7

*– Where is Mike?*

*– He may be at the café.*

8

*– Sit at this table, please.*

*– Thank you. May I place my books on that table?*

*– Yes, you may.*

*– May Alexander sit at his table?*

*– Yes, he may.*

9

*– May I sit on her bed?*

*– No, you must not.*

*– May Linda take his CD player?*

*– No. She must not take his CD player.*

*– May they take her map?*

*– No, they may not.*

10

– Du darfst dich nicht auf ihr Bett setzen.

– Sie darf seinen CD-Spieler nicht nehmen.

– Sie dürfen diese Notizbücher nicht nehmen.

*10*

*– You must not sit on her bed.*

*– She must not take his CD player.*

*– They must not take these notebooks.*

11

– Ich muss zur Bank gehen.

– Musst du jetzt gehen?

– Ja.

*11*

*– I must go to the bank.*

*– Must you go now?*

*– Yes, I must.*

12

– Musst du Englisch lernen?

– Ich muss nicht Englisch lernen. Ich muss Deutsch lernen.

*12*

*– Must you learn English?*

*– I need not learn English. I must learn German.*

13

– Muss sie zur Bank gehen?

– Nein, sie muss nicht zur Bank gehen.

*13*

*– Must she go to the bank?*

*– No. She need not go to the bank.*

14

– Darf ich dieses Fahrrad nehmen?

– Nein, du darfst dieses Fahrrad nicht nehmen.

*14*

*– May I take this bike?*

*– No, you must not take this bike.*

15

– Dürfen wir diese Notizbücher auf ihr Bett legen?

– Nein, ihr dürft die Notizbücher nicht auf ihr Bett legen.

*15*

*– May we place these notebooks on her bed?*

*– No. You must not place the notebooks on her bed.*

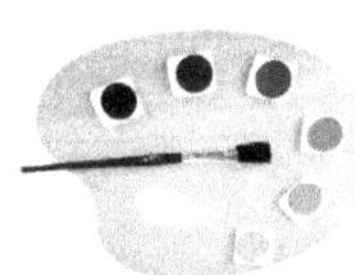

# 5

## Mike wohnt jetzt in Deutschland

*Mike lives in Germany now*

## A

### Vokabeln

*Words*

1. acht - eight
2. der Bauernhof - farm
3. brauchen - need
4. dort - there
5. drei - three
6. ein paar - some
7. essen - to eat
8. das Frühstück - breakfast;
   frühstücken - to have breakfast
9. fünf - five
10. gut - good, well
11. hören - to listen;
    Ich höre Musik. - I listen to music.
12. das Mädchen - girl
13. die Menschen - people
14. die Möbel - furniture
15. mögen, lieben - to like, to love
16. die Musik - music

17. der Platz - square
18. sechs - six
19. sieben - seven
20. der Stuhl - chair

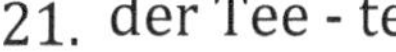

21. der Tee - tea
22. trinken - to drink
23. wollen - to want
24. die Zeitung - newspaper

## B

### **Mike wohnt jetzt in Deutschland**

1

Linda liest gut Deutsch. Ich lese auch Deutsch. Die Studenten gehen in den Park. Sie geht auch in den Park.

2

Wir wohnen in Bremerhaven. Alexander wohnt jetzt auch in Bremerhaven. Sein Vater und seine Mutter leben in der Schweiz. Mike wohnt jetzt in Bremerhaven. Sein Vater und seine Mutter leben in den USA.

3

Die Studenten spielen Tennis. Alexander spielt gut. Mike spielt nicht gut.

4

Wir trinken Tee. Linda trinkt grünen Tee. Stefan trinkt schwarzen Tee. Ich trinke auch schwarzen Tee.

5

Ich höre Musik. Sarah hört auch Musik. Sie hört gerne gute Musik.

6

Ich brauche sechs Notizbücher. Stefan braucht sieben Notizbücher. Linda braucht acht Notizbücher.

7

Sarah will etwas trinken. Ich will auch etwas trinken. Alexander will etwas essen.

### ***Mike lives in Germany now***

*1*

*Linda reads German well. I read German too. The students go to the park. She goes to the park too.*

*2*

*We live in Bremerhaven. Alexander lives in Bremerhaven now too. His father and mother live in Switzerland. Mike lives in Bremerhaven now. His father and mother live in USA.*

*3*

*The students play tennis. Alexander plays well. Mike does not play well.*

*4*

*We drink tea. Linda drinks green tea. Stefan drinks black tea. I drink black tea too.*

*5*

*I listen to music. Sarah listens to music too. She likes to listen to good music.*

*6*

*I need six notebooks. Stefan needs seven notebooks. Linda needs eight notebooks*

*7*

*Sarah wants to drink. I want to drink too. Alexander wants to eat.*

8

Dort liegt eine Zeitung auf dem Tisch. Alexander nimmt sie und liest. Er liest gerne Zeitung.

*8*

*There is a newspaper on the table. Alexander takes it and reads. He likes to read newspapers.*

9

Im Zimmer gibt es Möbel. Es gibt dort sechs Tische und sechs Stühle.

*9*

*There is some furniture in the room. There are six tables and six chairs there.*

10

Es sind drei Mädchen im Zimmer. Sie frühstücken. Sarah isst Brot und trinkt Tee. Sie mag grünen Tee.

*10*

*There are three girls in the room. They are eating breakfast. Sarah is eating bread and drinking tea. She likes green tea.*

11

Auf dem Tisch liegen ein paar Bücher. Sie sind nicht neu. Sie sind alt.

*11*

*There are some books on the table. They are not new. They are old.*

12

- Ist in dieser Straße eine Bank?

- Ja. Es gibt fünf Banken in dieser Straße. Sie sind nicht groß.

*12*

*- Is there a bank in this street?*

*- Yes, there is. There are five banks in this street. The banks are not big.*

13

- Sind Menschen auf dem Platz?

- Ja, auf dem Platz sind ein paar Menschen.

*13*

*- Are there people in the square?*

*- Yes, there are. There are some people in the square.*

14

- Stehen Fahrräder vor dem Café?

- Ja, es stehen vier Fahrräder vor dem Café. Sie sind nicht neu.

*14*

*- Are there bikes at the café?*

*- Yes, there are. There are four bikes at the café. They are not new.*

15

- Gibt es in dieser Straße ein Hotel?

- Nein, es gibt keine Hotels in dieser Straße.

*15*

*- Is there a hotel in this street?*

*- No, there is not. There are no hotels in this street.*

16

- Gibt es in dieser Straße große Läden?

- Nein, es gibt keine großen Läden in dieser Straße.

*16*

*- Are there any big shops in that street?*

*- No, there are not. There are no big shops in that street.*

17

- Gibt es in Deutschland Bauernhöfe?

- Ja, es gibt viele Bauernhöfe in Deutschland.

*17*

*- Are there any farms in Germany?*

*- Yes, there are. There are many farms in Germany.*

18

- Sind Möbel in diesem Zimmer?

- Ja, es sind dort vier Tische und einige Stühle.

*18*

*- Is there any furniture in that room?*

*- Yes, there is. There are four tables and some chairs there.*

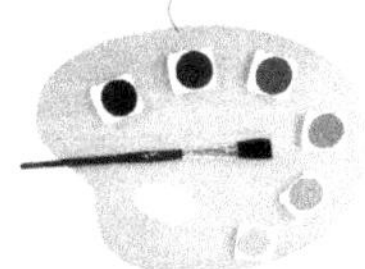

# 6

## Mike hat viele Freunde

*Mike has many friends*

### A

**Vokabeln**

*Words*

1. die Agentur - agency
2. die Arbeit - job
3. die Arbeitsvermittlung - job agency
4. auch - as well
5. das Auto - car
6. die CD - CD
7. der Computer - computer
8. frei - free
   die Freizeit, freie Zeit - free time
9. der Freund - friend
10. in - into
11. der Kaffee - coffee
12. kennen - to know
13. der Koch/die Köchin - cooker
14. kommen - come, go

15. sauber - clean
16. Stefans Buch - Stefan's book
17. die Tür - door
18. unter - under
19. der Vater - dad
20. viel, viele - much, many
21. viel zu tun haben - to have a lot of work

## B

**Mike hat viele Freunde**

1

Mike hat viele Freunde. Mikes Freunde gehen ins Café. Sie trinken gerne Kaffee. Mikes Freunde trinken viel Kaffee.

2

Alexanders Vater hat ein Auto. Das Auto seines Vaters ist sauber, aber alt. Alexanders Vater fährt viel Auto. Er hat eine gute Arbeit und im Moment viel zu tun.

3

Stefan hat viele CDs. Stefans CDs liegen auf seinem Bett. Stefans CD-Spieler ist auch auf seinem Bett.

4

Mike liest deutsche Zeitungen. Auf dem Tisch in Mikes Zimmer liegen viele Zeitungen.

5

Anke hat eine Katze und einen Hund. Ankes Katze ist im Zimmer unter dem Bett. Ankes Hund ist auch im Zimmer.

6

In dem Auto ist ein Mann. Der Mann hat eine Karte. Die Karte des Mannes ist groß. Dieser Mann fährt viel Auto.

7

Ich bin Student. Ich habe viel Freizeit.

Ich gehe zu einer Arbeitsvermittlung. Ich brauche

***Mike has many friends***

*1*

*Mike has many friends. Mike's friends go to the café. They like to drink coffee. Mike's friends drink a lot of coffee.*

*2*

*Alexander's dad has a car. The dad's car is clean but old. Alexander's dad drives a lot. He has a good job and he has a lot of work now.*

*3*

*Stefan has a lot of CDs. Stefan's CDs are on his bed. Stefan's CD player is on his bed as well.*

*4*

*Mike reads German newspapers. There are many newspapers on the table in Mike's room.*

*5*

*Anke has a cat and a dog. Anke's cat is in the room under the bed. Anke's dog is in the room as well.*

*6*

*There is a man in this car. This man has a map. The man's map is big. This man drives a lot.*

*7*

*I am a student. I have a lot of free time.*

*I go to a job agency. I need a good job.*

einen guten Job.

*Alexander and Mike have a little free time. They go to the job agency as well.*

Alexander und Mike haben ein bisschen freie Zeit. Sie gehen auch zu der Arbeitsvermittlung.

*Alexander has a computer. The agency may give Alexander a good job.*

Alexander hat einen Computer. Die Agentur wird ihm vielleicht eine gute Arbeit geben.

8

Linda hat eine neue Köchin. Lindas Köchin ist gut und sauber. Sie macht Frühstück für Lindas Kinder. Anke und Stefan sind Lindas Kinder. Lindas Kinder trinken viel Tee. Die Mutter trinkt ein bisschen Kaffee. Ankes Mutter kann nur ein paar Wörter auf Englisch. Sie spricht sehr wenig Englisch. Linda hat Arbeit. Sie hat wenig Freizeit.

*8*

*Linda has a new cooker. Linda's cooker is good and clean. She cooks breakfast for her children. Anke and Stefan are Linda's children. Linda's children drink a lot of tea. The mother drinks a little coffee. Anke's mother can speak very few English words. She speaks English very little. Linda has a job. She has little free time.*

9

Mike spricht wenig Deutsch. Er kennt nur sehr wenige deutsche Wörter. Ich kenne viele deutsche Wörter. Ich spreche ein bisschen Deutsch. Diese Frau kennt viele deutsche Wörter. Sie spricht gut Deutsch.

*9*

*Mike can speak German little. Mike knows very few German words. I know a lot of German words. I can speak German a little. This woman knows many German words. She can speak German well.*

10

Elmar arbeitet in einer Arbeitsvermittlung. Diese Arbeitsvermittlung ist in Bremerhaven. Elmar hat ein Auto. Elmars Auto steht an der Straße. Elmar hat viel Arbeit. Er muss in die Agentur gehen. Er fährt mit dem Auto dorthin. Elmar kommt in die Agentur. Dort sind viele Studenten. Sie brauchen Arbeit. Elmars Arbeit ist, den Studenten zu helfen.

*10*

*Elmar works at a job agency. This job agency is in Bremerhaven. Elmar has a car. Elmar's car is in the street. Elmar has a lot of work. He must go to the agency. He drives there. Elmar comes into the agency. There are a lot of students there. They need jobs. Elmar's job is to help the students.*

11

Vor dem Hotel steht ein Auto. Die Türen des Autos sind nicht sauber.

*11*

*There is a car at the hotel. The doors of this car are not clean.*

In diesem Hotel wohnen viele Studenten. Die Zimmer des Hotels sind klein, aber sauber. Das ist Mikes Zimmer. Das Fenster des Zimmers ist groß und sauber.

*Many students live in this hotel. The rooms of the hotel are little but clean. This is Mike's room. The window of the room is big and clean.*

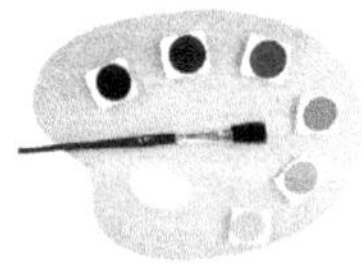

# 7

## Stefan kauft ein Fahrrad

*Stefan buys a bike*

## A

### Vokabeln

Words

1. der Arbeiter - worker
2. das Bad, das Badezimmer - bathroom; die Badewanne - bath
3. der Badezimmertisch - bathroom table
4. das Büro - office
5. der Bus - bus
   mit dem Bus fahren - to go by bus
6. dann - then

   danach - after that
7. einer nach dem anderen - one by one
8. Fahrrad fahren, mit dem Fahrrad fahren - to go by bike, to ride a bike
9. die Firma - firm

   die Firmen - firms
10. das Gesicht - face
11. heute - today
12. der Imbiss - snack

13. die Küche - kitchen
14. machen - to make
    die Kaffeemaschine - coffee-maker
15. mit - with
16. der Morgen - morning
17. der Samstag - Saturday
18. die Schlange - queue
19. der Sport - sport;
    das Sportgeschäft - sport shop,
    das Sportfahrrad - sport bike
20. waschen - to wash
21. die Waschmaschine - washer
22. die Zeit - time
23. das Zentrum - centre
    das Stadtzentrum - city centre
24. das Zuhause - home
    nach Hause gehen - go home

# B

## Stefan kauft ein Fahrrad

Es ist Samstagmorgen. Stefan geht ins Bad. Das Badezimmer ist nicht groß. Dort gibt es eine Badewanne, eine Waschmaschine und einen Badezimmertisch. Stefan wäscht sich das Gesicht. Dann geht er in die Küche. Auf dem Küchentisch steht ein Teekessel. Stefan frühstückt. Stefans Frühstück ist nicht groß. Dann macht er Kaffee mit der Kaffeemaschine und trinkt ihn. Er will heute in ein Sportgeschäft. Stefan geht auf die Straße. Er nimmt den Bus 7. Stefan braucht nicht lange, um mit dem Bus zum Laden zu fahren.

Stefan geht in das Sportgeschäft. Er will sich ein neues Sportfahrrad kaufen. Es gibt viele Sportfahrräder. Sie sind schwarz, blau und grün. Stefan mag blaue Fahrräder. Er will ein blaues kaufen. Im Laden ist eine Schlange. Stefan braucht lange, um das Fahrrad zu kaufen. Dann geht er auf die Straße und fährt mit dem Fahrrad. Er fährt ins Stadtzentrum. Dann fährt er vom Zentrum in den Stadtpark. Es ist so schön, mit einem neuen Sportfahrrad zu fahren!

Es ist Samstagmorgen, aber Elmar ist in seinem Büro. Er hat heute viel zu tun. Vor Elmars Büro ist eine Schlange. In der Schlange stehen viele Studenten und Arbeiter. Sie brauchen Arbeit.

## *Stefan buys a bike*

*It is Saturday morning. Stefan goes to the bathroom. The bathroom is not big. There is a bath, a washer and a bathroom table there. Stefan washes his face. Then he goes to the kitchen. There is a tea-maker on the kitchen table. Stefan eats his breakfast. Stefan's breakfast is not big. Then he makes some coffee with the coffee-maker and drinks it. He wants to go to a sport shop today. Stefan goes into the street. He takes bus seven. It takes Stefan a little time to go to the shop by bus.*

*Stefan goes into the sport shop. He wants to buy a new sport bike. There are a lot of sport bikes there. They are black, blue and green. Stefan likes blue bikes. He wants to buy a blue one. There is a queue in the shop. It takes Stefan a lot of time to buy the bike. Then he goes to the street and rides the bike. He rides to the city centre. Then he rides from the city centre to the city park. It is so nice to ride a new sport bike!*

*It is Saturday morning but Elmar is in his office. He has a lot of work today. There is a queue to Elmar's office. There are many students and workers in the queue. They*

Sie gehen einer nach dem anderen in Elmars Büro. Sie sprechen mit Elmar. Dann gibt er ihnen Adressen von Firmen.

*need a job. They go one by one into Elmar's room. They speak with Elmar. Then he gives addresses of firms.*

Jetzt ist Zeit für einen Imbiss. Elmar macht Kaffee mit der Kaffeemaschine. Er isst seinen Imbiss und trinkt Kaffee. Jetzt ist keine Schlange mehr vor seinem Büro. Elmar kann nach Hause gehen. Er geht auf die Straße. Es ist so ein schöner Tag! Elmar geht nach Hause. Er holt seine Kinder ab und geht in den Stadtpark. Dort haben sie eine schöne Zeit.

*It is snack time now. Elmar makes some coffee with the coffee maker. He eats his snack and drinks some coffee. There is no queue to his office now. Elmar can go home. He goes into the street. It is so nice today! Elmar goes home. He takes his children and goes to the city park. They have a nice time there.*

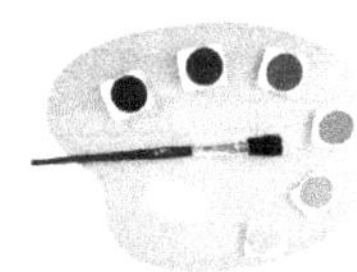

# 8

## Linda will eine neue DVD kaufen

*Linda wants to buy a new DVD*

# A

### Vokabeln

*Words*

1. das Abenteuer - adventure
2. als - than; Elmar ist älter als Linda. - Elmar is older than Linda.
3. bitten, fragen - to ask
4. dass - that; Ich weiß, dass dieses Buch interessant ist. - I know that this book is interesting.
5. dauern - to last, to take; Der Film dauert mehr als 3 Stunden - The movie is more than three hours long
6. die DVD - DVD
7. der Film - film
8. freundlich - friendly
9. fünfzehn - fifteen
10. geben - to hand
11. groß-größer-am größten - big-bigger-biggest
12. interessant - interesting
13. jung - young

14. die Kiste - box

15. lang- long

16. Lieblings- - favourite; der Lieblingsfilm - favourite film

17. mehr - more

18. sagen - to say

19. die Stunde - hour

20. die Tasse - cup

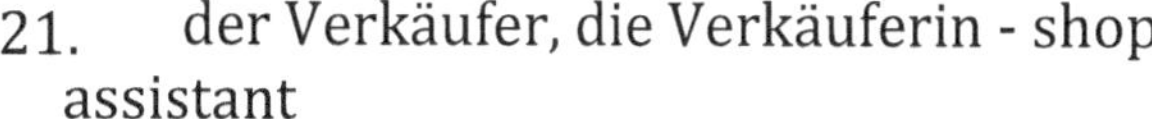

21. der Verkäufer, die Verkäuferin - shop assistant

22. die Videokassette - videocassette

23. die Videothek - video-shop

24. weggehen - to go away

25. zeigen - to show

26. zwanzig - twenty

## B

### Linda will eine neue DVD kaufen

Stefan und Anke sind Lindas Kinder. Anke ist die Jüngste. Sie ist fünf. Stefan ist fünfzehn Jahre älter als Anke. Er ist zwanzig. Anke ist viel jünger als Stefan.

Anke, Linda und Stefan sind in der Küche. Sie trinken Tee. Ankes Tasse ist groß. Lindas Tasse ist größer. Stefans Tasse ist am größten.

Linda hat viele Videokassetten und DVDs mit interessanten Filmen. Sie will einen neueren Film kaufen. Sie geht in eine Videothek. Dort sind viele Kisten mit Videokassetten und DVDs. Sie bittet einen Verkäufer, ihr zu helfen. Der Verkäufer gibt Linda ein paar Filme. Linda will mehr über diese Filme wissen, aber der Verkäufer geht weg.

Es gibt eine andere Verkäuferin im Laden und sie ist freundlicher. Sie fragt Linda nach ihren Lieblingsfilmen. Linda mag romantische Filme und Abenteuerfilme. Der Film „Titanic“ ist ihr Lieblingsfilm. Die Verkäuferin zeigt Linda eine DVD mit dem neusten Hollywoodfilm „Der deutsche Freund“. Er handelt von den romantischen Abenteuern eines Mannes und einer jungen Frau in Deutschland.

Sie zeigt Linda auch eine DVD mit dem Film

### *Linda wants to buy a new DVD*

*Stefan and Anke are Linda’s children. Anke is the youngest child. She is five years old. Stefan is fifteen years older than Anke. He is twenty. Anke is much younger than Stefan.*

*Anke, Linda and Stefan are in the kitchen. They drink tea. Anke’s cup is big. Linda’s cup is bigger. Stefan’s cup is the biggest.*

*Linda has a lot of videocassettes and DVDs with interesting films. She wants to buy a newer film. She goes to a video-shop. There are many boxes with videocassettes and DVDs there. She asks a shop assistant to help her. The shop assistant hands Linda some cassettes. Linda wants to know more about these films but the shop assistant goes away.*

*There is one more shop assistant in the shop and she is friendlier. She asks Linda about her favorite films. Linda likes romantic films and adventure films. The film "Titanic" is her favorite film. The shop assistant shows Linda a DVD with the newest Hollywood film "The German Friend". It is about romantic adventures of a man and a young woman in Germany.*

*She shows Linda a DVD with the film "The*

„Die Firma". Die Verkäuferin sagt, dass der Film „Die Firma" einer der interessantesten Filme ist. Und auch einer der längsten. Er dauert mehr als drei Stunden. Linda mag längere Filme. Sie sagt, dass „Titanic" der interessanteste und der längste Film ist, den sie hat. Linda kauft die DVD mit dem Film „Die Firma". Sie bedankt sich bei der Verkäuferin und geht.

*Firm" as well. The shop assistant says that the film "The Firm" is one of the most interesting films. And it is one of the longest films as well. It is more than three hours long. Linda likes longer films. She says that "Titanic" is the most interesting and the longest film that she has. Linda buys a DVD with the film "The Firm". She thanks the shop assistant and goes.*

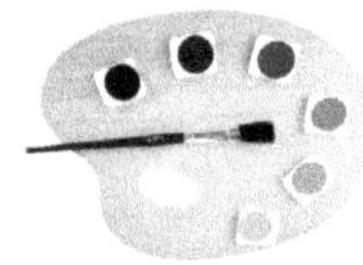

# 9

## Alexander hört amerikanische Musik

*Alexander listens to American songs*

## A

### Vokabeln

*Words*

1. anfangen - to begin
2. anrufen - to call on the phone;

   rufen - call;
   das Callcenter - call centre
3. außer Betrieb - out of order
4. das Brot - bread
5. die Butter - butter
6. einfach - simple
7. etwa - about
8. die Familie - family
9. gefallen - to like;
   Das gefällt mir. - I like that.

10. der Hut - hat
11. jeder, jede, jedes - every
12. der Kopf - head;
    gehen - to head, to go
13. die Minute - minute
14. die Nähe - nearness
    in der Nähe - near, nearby, next
15. der Name - name;
    nennen - to name
16. rennen, joggen, laufen - to run
17. der Sänger - singer
18. der Satz - phrase
19. sich schämen - to be ashamed;
    er schämt sich - he is ashamed
20. sehr - very
21. singen - sing
22. springen - to jump;
    der Sprung - jump
23. das Studentenwohnheim - dorms
24. der Tag - day
25. die Tasche - bag
26. das Telefon - telephone;
    telefonieren - to telephone
27. vor - before
28. weil - because

 **B**

### Alexander hört amerikanische Musik

Carol ist Studentin. Sie ist zwanzig. Carol kommt aus den USA. Sie wohnt im Studentenwohnheim. Sie ist ein sehr nettes Mädchen. Carol hat ein blaues Kleid an. Auf dem Kopf hat sie einen Hut.

Carol will heute ihre Familie anrufen. Sie geht ins Callcenter, weil ihr Telefon außer Betrieb ist. Das Callcenter ist vor dem Café. Carol ruft ihre Familie an. Sie spricht mit ihrer Mutter und ihrem Vater. Der Anruf dauert etwa fünf Minuten. Dann ruft sie ihre Freundin Angela an. Dieser Anruf dauert etwa drei Minuten.

Mike mag Sport. Er geht jeden Morgen im Park in der Nähe des Studentenwohnheims joggen. Heute läuft er auch. Er springt auch. Er springt sehr weit. Alexander und Stefan laufen und springen mit Mike. Stefan springt weiter. Alexander springt am weitesten. Er springt am besten von allen. Dann laufen Mike und

### Alexander listens to American songs

*Carol is a student. She is twenty years old. Carol is from the USA. She lives in the student dorms. She is a very nice girl. Carol has a blue dress on. There is a hat on her head.*

*Carol wants to telephone her family today. She heads to the call centre because her telephone is out of order. The call centre is in front of the café. Carol calls her family. She speaks with her mother and father. The call takes her about five minutes. Then she calls her friend Angela. This call takes her about three minutes.*

*Mike likes sport. He runs every morning in the park near the dorms. He is running today too. He jumps as well. His jumps are very long. Alexander and Stefan run and jump with Mike. Stefan's jumps are longer. Alexander's jumps are the longest. He jumps best of all. Then Mike and Alexander run to*

Alexander zum Studentenwohnheim und Stefan nach Hause.

*the dorms and Stefan runs home.*

Mike frühstückt in seinem Zimmer. Er holt Brot und Butter. Er macht Kaffee mit der Kaffeemaschine. Dann bestreicht er das Brot mit Butter und isst.

*Mike has his breakfast in his room. He takes bread and butter. He makes some coffee with the coffee-maker. Then he butters the bread and eats.*

Mike wohnt im Studentenwohnheim in Bremerhaven. Sein Zimmer ist in der Nähe von Alexanders Zimmer. Mikes Zimmer ist nicht groß. Es ist sauber, weil Mike es jeden Tag sauber macht. In seinem Zimmer stehen ein Tisch, ein Bett, ein paar Stühle und ein paar andere Möbel. Mikes Bücher und Notizbücher liegen auf dem Tisch. Seine Tasche ist unter dem Tisch. Die Stühle stehen am Tisch. Mike nimmt ein paar CDs in die Hand und geht zu Alexanders Zimmer, weil Alexander amerikanische Musik hören will.

*Mike lives in the dorms in Bremerhaven. His room is near Alexander's room. Mike's room is not big. It is clean because Mike cleans it every day. There is a table, a bed, some chairs and some more furniture in his room. Mike's books and notebooks are on the table. His bag is under the table. The chairs are at the table. Mike takes some CDs in his hand and heads to Alexander's because Alexander wants to listen to American music.*

Alexander sitzt in seinem Zimmer am Tisch. Seine Katze ist unter dem Tisch. Vor der Katze liegt etwas Brot. Die Katze isst das Brot. Mike gibt Alexander die CDs. Auf den CDs ist die beste amerikanische Musik. Alexander will auch die Namen der amerikanischen Sänger wissen. Mike nennt seine Lieblingssänger. Er nennt Avril Lavigne, Madonna, Mark Anthony und Jennifer López. Diese Namen sind Alexander neu.

*Alexander is in his room at the table. His cat is under the table. There is some bread before the cat. The cat eats the bread. Mike hands the CDs to Alexander. There is the best American music on the CDs. Alexander wants to know the names of the American singers as well. Mike names his favorite singers. He names Avril Lavigne, Madonna, Mike Anthony, and Jennifer López. These names are new to Alexander.*

Er hört die CDs an und beginnt dann, die amerikanischen Lieder zu singen. Ihm gefallen die Lieder sehr. Alexander bittet Mike, den Text der Lieder aufzuschreiben. Mike schreibt die Texte der besten amerikanischen Lieder für Alexander auf. Alexander sagt, dass er die Texte von ein paar Liedern lernen will, und bittet Mike um Hilfe. Mike hilft Alexander, die amerikanischen Texte zu lernen. Es dauert sehr lange, weil Mike nicht gut Deutsch spricht. Mike schämt sich. Er kann nicht mal ein paar einfache Sätze sagen! Dann geht Mike in sein Zimmer und lernt Deutsch.

*He listens to the CDs and then begins to sing the American songs! He likes these songs very much. Alexander asks Mike to write the words of the songs. Mike writes the words of the best American songs for Alexander. Alexander says that he wants to learn the words of some songs and asks Mike to help. Mike helps Alexander to learn the American words. It takes a lot of time because Mike cannot speak German well. Mike is ashamed. He cannot say some simple phrases! Then Mike goes to his room and learns German.*

# 10

## Alexander kauft Fachbücher über Design

*Alexander buys textbooks on design*

## A

### Vokabeln

*Words*

1. die Art - kind, type
2. die Aufgabe, Lektion - lesson
3. das Design - design
4. erklären - to explain
5. das Fachbuch - textbook
6. das Foto - picture
7. gut - fine
8. hallo - hello
9. ihm - him
10. irgendwelche - any
11. kosten - to cost
12. die Muttersprache - native language
13. nur - only
14. das Programm - program

15. schauen, betrachten - to look
16. sehen - to see
17. die Sprache - language
18. studieren - to study
19. tschüss - bye

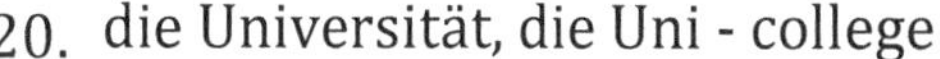

20. die Universität, die Uni - college
21. wählen, aussuchen - to choose
22. zahlen - to pay
23. wirklich - really

## B

### Alexander kauft Fachbücher über Design

Alexander ist Schweizer und seine Muttersprache ist Französisch. Er studiert Design an der Universität in Bremerhaven.

Heute ist Samstag und Alexander hat viel Freizeit. Er will ein paar Bücher über Design kaufen. Er geht zum Buchladen in der Nähe. Der könnte Fachbücher über Design haben. Er kommt in den Laden und betrachtet den Tisch mit Büchern. Eine Frau kommt zu Alexander. Sie ist eine Verkäuferin.

„Hallo, kann ich Ihnen helfen?“, fragt ihn die Verkäuferin.

„Hallo“, sagt Alexander. „Ich studiere Design an der Universität. Ich brauche ein paar Fachbücher. Haben Sie irgendwelche Fachbücher über Design?“, fragt Alexander sie.

„Welche Art von Design? Wir haben Fachbücher über Möbeldesign, Autodesign, Sportdesign oder Internetdesign“, erklärt sie ihm.

„Können Sie mir Fachbücher über Möbeldesign und Internetdesign zeigen?“, fragt Alexander sie.

„Sie können sich Bücher von den nächsten Tischen aussuchen. Schauen Sie sie sich an. Dies ist ein Buch von dem italienischen Möbeldesigner Palatino. Dieser Designer erklärt das Design italienischer Möbel. Er erklärt auch europäisches und amerikanisches Möbeldesign.

### *Alexander buys textbooks on design*

*Alexander is Swiss and French is his native language. He studies design at college in Bremerhaven.*

*It is Saturday today and Alexander has a lot of free time. He wants to buy some books on design. He goes to the nearby book shop. They may have some textbooks on design. He comes into the shop and looks at the tables with books. A woman comes to Alexander. She is a shop assistant.*

*"Hello. Can I help you?" the shop assistant asks him.*

*"Hello," Alexander says. "I study design at college. I need some textbooks. Do you have any textbooks on design?" Alexander asks her.*

*"What kind of design? We have some textbooks on furniture design, car design, sport design, internet design," she explains to him.*

*"Can you show me some textbooks on furniture design and internet design?" Alexander says to her.*

*"You can choose the books from the next tables. Look at them. This is a book by Italian furniture designer Palatino. This designer explains the design of Italian furniture. He explains the furniture design of Europe and*

In dem Buch sind einige gute Bilder", erklärt die Verkäuferin.

„Ich sehe, dass das Buch auch Aufgaben enthält. Dieses Buch ist wirklich gut. Wie viel kostet es?", fragt Alexander sie.

„Es kostet 52 Euro. Und mit dem Buch kommt eine CD. Auf der CD ist ein Computerprogramm für Möbeldesign", sagt die Verkäuferin.

„Das gefällt mir wirklich", sagt Alexander.

„Dort können Sie sich ein paar Fachbücher über Internetdesign anschauen", erklärt ihm die Frau. „Dieses Buch ist über das Computerprogramm Microsoft Office. Und diese Bücher sind über das Computerprogramm Flash. Schauen Sie sich dieses rote Buch an. Es ist über Flash und es enthält einige interessante Lektionen. Suchen Sie sich eins aus."

„Wie viel kostet das rote Buch?", fragt Alexander sie.

„Dieses Buch mit zwei CDs kostet nur 43 Euro", sagt die Verkäuferin.

„Ich möchte das Buch von Palatino über Möbeldesign und das rote Buch über Flash kaufen. Wie viel muss ich dafür zahlen?", fragt Alexander.

„Sie müssen 95 Euro für diese zwei Bücher zahlen", sagt die Verkäuferin.

Alexander zahlt. Dann nimmt er die Bücher und die CDs.

„Tschüss", sagt die Verkäuferin zu ihm.

„Tschüss", sagt Alexander und geht.

*the USA as well. There are some fine pictures there," the shop assistant explains.*

*"I see there are some lessons in the book too. This book is really fine. How much is it?" Alexander asks her.*

*"It costs 52 euros. And with the book you have a CD. There is a computer program for furniture design on the CD," the shop assistant says to him.*

*"I really like it," Alexander says.*

*"You can see some textbooks on internet design there," the woman explains to him. "This book is about the computer program Microsoft Office. And these books are about the computer program Flash. Look at this red book. It is about Flash and it has some interesting lessons. Choose, please."*

*"How much is this red book?" Alexander asks her.*

*"This book, with two CDs, costs only 43 euros," the shop assistant says to him.*

*"I want to buy this book by Palatino about furniture design and this red book about Flash. How much must I pay for them?" Alexander asks.*

*"You need to pay 95 euros for these two books," the shop assistant says to him.*

*Alexander pays. Then he takes the books and the CDs.*

*"Bye," the shop assistant says to him.*

*"Bye," Alexander says to her and goes.*

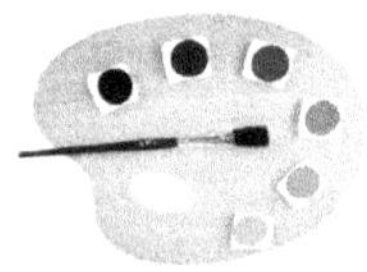

# 11

## Mike will ein bisschen Geld verdienen (Teil 1)

*Mike wants to earn some money (part 1)*

## A

### Vokabeln

*Words*

1. die Antwort - answer,
   antworten - to answer
2. antworten, erwidern - answer
3. beladen - to load,
   der Verlader - loader
4. besser - better
5. die Energie - energy
6. das Ende - finish
   beenden - to finish
7. Fortsetzung folgt - to be continued
8. gut, alles klar - OK, well
9. die Kiste - box

10. der Lastwagen - truck
11. die Liste - list
12. nach - after
13. noch einen - one more
14. normal - usual
    normalerweise - usually
15. die Notiz - note
16. die Nummer - number
17. die Personalabteilung - personnel department
18. schnell - quick, quickly
19. schwer - hard
20. die Stunde - hour
    stündlich - hourly
21. der Tag - day
    täglich, jeden Tag - daily
22. der Teil - part
23. der Transport - transport
24. Uhr - o'clock
    Es ist zwei Uhr. - It is two o'clock.
25. verdienen - to earn
    Ich verdiene 10 Euro pro Stunde - I earn 10 euros per hour.
26. verstehen - to understand

## B

**Mike will ein bisschen Geld verdienen (Teil 1)**

Mike hat jeden Tag nach der Universität freie Zeit. Er will ein bisschen Geld verdienen. Er geht in eine Arbeitsvermittlung. Sie geben ihm die Adresse einer Transportfirma. Die Transportfirma *Rapid* braucht einen Verlader. Diese Arbeit ist wirklich schwer. Aber sie bezahlen 11 Euro pro Stunde. Mike will den Job annehmen. Also geht er zum Büro der Transportfirma.„Hallo. Ich habe eine Notiz für Sie von einer Arbeitsvermittlung“, sagt Mike zu einer Frau in der Personalabteilung der Firma. Er gibt ihr die Notiz.

„Hallo“, sagt die Frau. „Ich bin Isolde Pohl. Ich bin die Leiterin der Personalabteilung. Wie heißen Sie?“

„Ich heiße Mike Sullivan“, sagt Mike.

„Sind Sie Deutscher?“, fragt Isolde.

„Nein, ich bin Amerikaner“, antwortet Mike.

***Mike wants to earn some money (part 1)***

*Mike has free time daily after college. He wants to earn some money. He heads to a job agency. They give him the address of a transport firm. The transport firm Rapid needs a loader. This work is really hard. But they pay 11 euros per hour. Mike wants to take this job. So he goes to the office of the transport firm.*

*"Hello. I have a note for you from a job agency," Mike says to a woman in the personnel department of the firm. He gives her the note.*

*"Hello," the woman says. "My name is Isolde Pohl. I am the head of the personnel department. What is your name?"*

*"My name is Mike Sullivan," Mike says.*

*"Are you German?" Isolde asks.*

*"No. I am American," Mike answers.*

„Können Sie gut Deutsch sprechen und schreiben?", fragt sie.

*"Can you speak and read German well?" she asks.*

„Ja", sagt er.

*"Yes, I can," he says.*

„Wie alt sind Sie?", fragt sie.

*"How old are you, Mike?" she asks.*

„Ich bin zwanzig", antwortet Mike.

*"I am twenty years old," Mike answers.*

„Wollen Sie in der Transportfirma als Verlader arbeiten?", fragt ihn die Leiterin der Personalabteilung.

*"Do you want to work at the transport firm as a loader?" the head of the personnel department asks him.*

Mike schämt sich, zu sagen, dass er keine bessere Arbeit haben kann, weil er nicht gut Deutsch spricht. Deswegen sagt er: „Ich möchte 11 Euro pro Stunde verdienen."

*Mike is ashamed to say that he cannot have a better job because he cannot speak German well. So he says: "I want to earn 11 euros per hour."*

„Na gut", sagt Isolde. „Normalerweise hat unsere Transportfirma nicht viel Verladearbeit. Aber gerade brauchen wir wirklich noch einen Verlader. Können Sie schnell Kisten mit 20 Kilogramm Ladung verladen?"

*"Well-well," Isolde says. "Our transport firm usually does not have much loading work. But now we really need one more loader. Can you load quickly boxes with 20 kilograms of load?"*

„Ja, das kann ich. Ich habe viel Energie", antwortet Mike.

*"Yes, I can. I have a lot of energy," Mike answers.*

„Wir brauchen einen Verlader für drei Stunden täglich. Können Sie von vier bis sieben Uhr arbeiten?", fragt sie.

*"We need a loader daily for three hours. Can you work from four to seven o'clock?" she asks.*

„Ja, mein Unterricht endet um ein Uhr", antwortet der Student.

*"Yes, my lessons finish at one o'clock," the student answers to her.*

„Wann können Sie anfangen, zu arbeiten?", fragt ihn die Leiterin der Personalabteilung.

*"When can you begin the work?" the head of the personnel department asks him.*

„Ich kann jetzt anfangen", erwidert Mike.

*"I can begin now," Mike answers.*

„Gut. Schauen Sie sich diese Ladeliste an. Dort stehen Namen von Firmen und Läden", erklärt Isolde. „Bei jeder Firma und jedem Laden stehen ein paar Nummern. Das sind die Nummern der Kisten. Und das sind die Nummern der Lastwägen, auf die Sie die Kisten laden müssen. Die Lastwägen kommen und gehen stündlich. Sie müssen also schnell arbeiten. Alles klar?"

*"Well. Look at this loading list. There are some names of firms and shops in the list," Isolde explains. "Every firm and shop has some numbers. They are numbers of the boxes. And these are numbers of the trucks where you must load these boxes. The trucks come and go hourly. So you need to work quickly. OK?"*

„Alles klar", antwortet Mike, ohne Isolde richtig zu verstehen.

*"OK," Mike answers, not understanding Isolde well.*

„Nehmen Sie jetzt diese Ladeliste und gehen Sie

*"Now take this loading list and go to the loading door number three," the head of the*

zur Ladetür Nummer drei“, sagt die Leiterin der Personalabteilung zu Mike. Mike nimmt die Ladeliste und geht arbeiten.

(Fortsetzung folgt)

*personnel department says to Mike. Mike takes the loading list and goes to work.*

*(to be continued)*

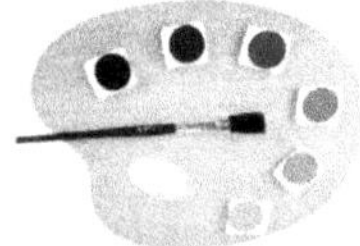

# 12

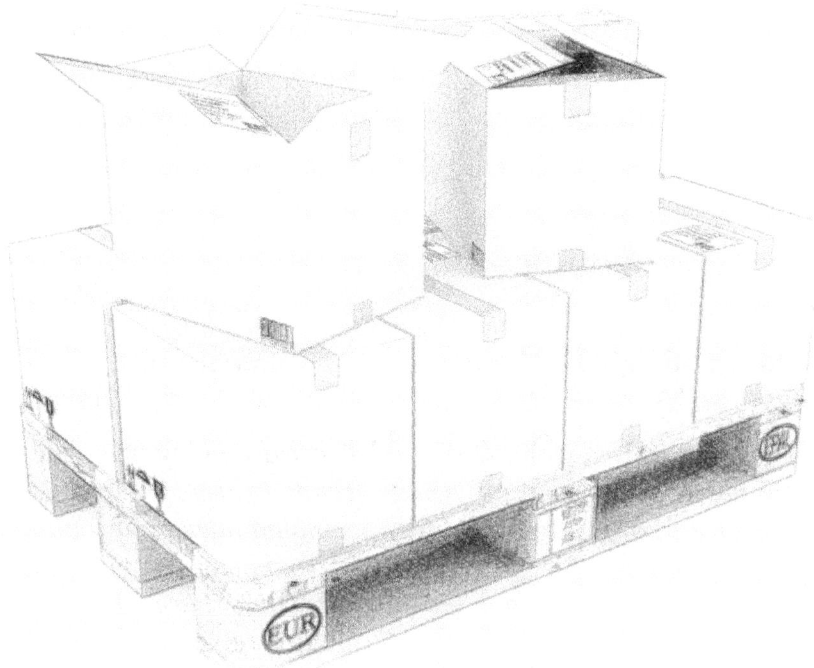


## Mike will ein bisschen Geld verdienen (Teil 2)

*Mike wants to earn some money (part 2)*

## A

### Vokabeln

*Words*

1. anstelle von - instead of
   an deiner Stelle - instead of you
2. aufstehen - to get up
   Steh auf! - Get up!
3. bringen - to bring
4. dein - your
5. fahren - to drive
   der Fahrer - driver
6. froh - glad
7. gehen - to walk
8. der Grund - reason
9. hassen - to hate

10. Herr, Hr. - mister, Mr.
11. hier (Ort) - here (a place),
    hierher (Richtung) - here (a direction),
    hier ist - here is
12. ihr - their
13. der Lehrer - teacher
14. leid tun - to be sorry
    Es tut mir leid. - I am sorry.
15. Mama, die Mutter - mom, mother
16. Montag - Monday
17. richtig - correct, correctly
    falsch - incorrectly
    korrigieren - to correct
18. schlecht - bad
19. der Sohn - son
20. treffen, kennenlernen - to meet
21. zurück - back

## B

### Mike will ein bisschen Geld verdienen (Teil 2)

An der Ladetür Nummer 3 stehen viele Lastwagen. Sie kommen mit ihrer Ladung zurück. Die Leiterin der Personalabteilung und der Firmenchef kommen dorthin. Sie gehen zu Mike. Mike lädt Kisten in einen Lastwagen. Er arbeitet schnell.

„Hey, Mike! Komm bitte hierher!", ruft Isolde. „Das ist der Chef der Firma, Hr. Klein."

„Es freut mich, Sie kennenzulernen", sagt Mike auf sie zugehend.

„Mich auch", antwortet Hr. Klein. „Wo ist Ihre Ladeliste?"

„Hier ist sie", Mike gibt ihm die Ladeliste.

„Na gut", sagt Hr. Klein, während er auf die Liste schaut. „Sehen Sie diese Lastwagen? Sie bringen ihre Fracht zurück, weil Sie die Kisten falsch verladen haben. Die Kisten mit Büchern werden zu einem Möbelladen gebracht anstelle von einem Buchladen, die Kisten mit Videos und DVDs zu einem Café anstelle von einer Videothek und die Kisten mit Sandwiches zu einer Videothek anstelle von einem Café! Das ist schlechte Arbeit! Es tut mir leid, aber Sie

### *Mike wants to earn some money (part 2)*

*There are many trucks at the loading door number three. They are coming back bringing back their loads. The head of the personnel department and the head of the firm come there. They come to Mike. Mike is loading boxes in a truck. He is working quickly.*

*"Hey, Mike! Please, come here," Isolde calls him. "This is the head of the firm, Mr. Klein."*

*"I am glad to meet you," Mike says coming to them.*

*"I too," Mr. Klein answers. "Where is your loading list?"*

*"It is here," Mike gives him the loading list.*

*"Well-well," Mr. Klein says looking in the list. "Look at these trucks. They are coming back bringing back their loads because you load the boxes incorrectly. The boxes with books go to a furniture shop instead of the book shop, the boxes with videocassettes and DVDs go to a café instead of the video shop, and the boxes with sandwiches go to a video shop instead of the café! It is bad work! Sorry*

können nicht in unserer Firma arbeiten", sagt Herr Klein und geht zurück in sein Büro.

*but you cannot work at our firm," Mr. Klein says and walks back to the office.*

Mike kann die Kisten nicht richtig verladen, weil er nur sehr wenig Deutsch lesen und verstehen kann. Isolde schaut ihn an. Mike schämt sich.

*Mike cannot load boxes correctly because he can read and understand very few German words. Isolde looks at him. Mike is ashamed.*

„Mike, du kannst dein Deutsch verbessern und dann wiederkommen, ok?", sagt Isolde.

*"Mike, you can learn German better and then come again. OK?" Isolde says.*

„Ok", antwortet Mike. „Tschüss Isolde."

*"OK," Mike answers. "Bye Isolde."*

„Tschüss Mike", antwortet Isolde.

*"Bye Mike," Isolde answers.*

Mike geht nach Hause. Er will jetzt sein Deutsch verbessern und sich dann eine neue Arbeit suchen.

*Mike walks home. He wants to learn German better now and then take a new job.*

## Es ist an der Zeit, in die Uni zu gehen

## *It is time to go to college*

An einem Montagmorgen kommt eine Mutter ins Zimmer, um ihren Sohn aufzuwecken.

*Monday morning a mother comes into the room to wake up her son.*

„Steh auf, es ist sieben Uhr. Es ist an der Zeit, in die Uni zu gehen!"

*"Get up, it is seven o'clock. It is time to go to college!"*

„Aber warum, Mama? Ich will nicht gehen."

*"But why, Mom? I don't want to go."*

„Nenne mir zwei Gründe, warum du nicht gehen willst", sagt die Mutter zu ihrem Sohn.

*"Name me two reasons why you don't want to go," the mother says to the son.*

„Die Studenten hassen mich und die Lehrer auch!"

*"The students hate me for one and the teachers hate me too!"*

„Oh, das sind keine Gründe, um nicht in die Uni zu gehen. Steh auf!"

*"Oh, they are not reasons not to go to college. Get up!"*

„Ok. Nenn mir zwei Gründe, warum ich in die Uni muss", sagt er zu seiner Mutter.

*"OK. Name me two reasons why I must go to college," he says to his mother.*

„Gut, einerseits, weil du 55 Jahre alt bist. Und andererseits, weil du der Direktor der Universität bist! Steh jetzt auf!"

*"Well, for one, you are 55 years old. And for two, you are the head of the college! Get up now!"*

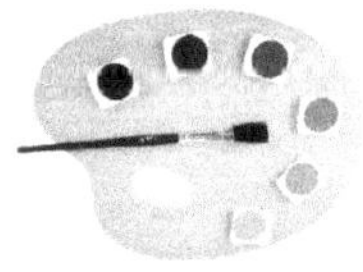

# A2 Level Course

# 13

## Der Name des Hotels

*The name of the hotel*

## A

**Vokabeln**

1. der Abend - evening
2. anderer - another
3. anhalten - to stop
4. der Aufzug - lift
5. die Brücke - bridge
6. dann - then
7. dumm - silly
8. finden - to find
9. der Fuß - foot
   zu Fuß - on foot
10. gehen - to walk
11. hindurch - through
12. jetzt, zurzeit, gerade - now
13. das Lächeln - smile
    lächeln - to smile
14. müde - tired
15. nach unten - down
16. die Nacht - night
17. öffnen - to open
18. Polen - Poland
19. rund - round
20. schlafen - to sleep

21. schon - already
22. der See - lake
23. sehen - to see
24. stehen - to stand
25. das Taxi - taxi
    der Taxifahrer - taxi driver
26. über - over, across
27. die Überraschung - surprise
    überraschen - to surprise
    überrascht, verwundert - surprised
28. vorbei - past
29. der Weg - way
30. die Werbung - advert
31. wieder - again
32. wütend - angry
33. weg - away
34. zeigen - to show

## B

### Der Name des Hotels

Das ist ein Student. Er heißt Kasper. Kasper kommt aus Polen. Er spricht kein Deutsch. Er will an einer Universität in Deutschland Deutsch lernen. Kasper wohnt zurzeit in einem Hotel in Bremerhaven.

Gerade ist er in seinem Zimmer. Er schaut auf die Karte. Diese Karte ist sehr gut. Kasper sieht Straßen, Plätze und Läden auf der Karte. Er geht aus dem Zimmer und durch den langen Gang zum Aufzug. Der Aufzug bringt ihn nach unten. Kasper geht durch die große Halle und aus dem Hotel. Er hält in der Nähe des Hotels an und schreibt den Namen des Hotels in sein Notizbuch.

Beim Hotel gibt es einen runden Platz und einen See. Kasper geht über den Platz zum See. Er geht um den See zur Brücke. Viele Autos, Lastwägen und Menschen überqueren die Brücke. Kasper geht unter der Brücke hindurch. Dann geht er eine Straße entlang zum Stadtzentrum. Er geht an vielen schönen Gebäuden vorbei.

Es ist schon Abend. Kasper ist müde und will zurück ins Hotel gehen. Er hält ein Taxi an,

### *The name of the hotel*

*This is a student. His name is Kasper. Kasper is from Poland. He cannot speak German. He wants to learn German at a college in Germany. Kasper lives in a hotel in Bremerhaven now.*

*He is in his room now. He is looking at the map. This map is very good. Kasper sees streets, squares and shops on the map. He goes out of the room and through the long corridor to the lift. The lift takes him down. Kasper goes through the big hall and out of the hotel. He stops near the hotel and writes the name of the hotel into his notebook.*

*There is a round square and a lake at the hotel. Kasper goes across the square to the lake. He walks round the lake to the bridge. Many cars, trucks and people go over the bridge. Kasper goes under the bridge. Then he walks along a street to the city centre. He goes past many nice buildings.*

*It is evening already. Kasper is tired and he wants to go back to the hotel. He stops a taxi,*

öffnet dann sein Notizbuch und zeigt dem Taxifahrer den Namen des Hotels. Der Taxifahrer schaut in das Notizbuch, lächelt und fährt weg. Kasper versteht nichts. Er steht da und schaut in sein Notizbuch. Dann hält er ein anderes Taxi an und zeigt dem Taxifahrer wieder den Namen des Hotels. Der Fahrer schaut in das Notizbuch. Dann schaut er Kasper an, lächelt und fährt auch weg.

*then opens his notebook and shows the name of the hotel to the taxi driver. The taxi driver looks in the notebook, smiles and drives away. Kasper cannot understand it. He stands and looks in his notebook. Then he stops another taxi and shows the name of the hotel to the taxi driver again. The driver looks in the notebook. Then he looks at Kasper, smiles and drives away too.*

Kasper ist verwundert. Er hält ein anderes Taxi an. Aber auch dieser Taxifahrer fährt weg. Kasper kann das nicht verstehen. Er ist verwundert und wütend. Aber er ist nicht dumm. Er öffnet seine Karte und findet den Weg zum Hotel. Er kehrt zu Fuß zum Hotel zurück.

*Kasper is surprised. He stops another taxi. But this taxi drives away too. Kasper cannot understand it. He is surprised and angry. But he is not silly. He opens his map and finds the way to the hotel. He comes back to the hotel on foot.*

Es ist Nacht. Kasper ist in seinem Bett. Er schläft. Die Sterne schauen durch das Fenster ins Zimmer. Das Notizbuch liegt auf dem Tisch. Es ist offen. „Ford ist das beste Auto“. Das ist nicht der Name des Hotels. Das ist Werbung am Hotelgebäude.

*It is night. Kasper is in his bed. He is sleeping. The stars are looking into the room through the window. The notebook is on the table. It is open. "Ford is the best car". This is not the name of the hotel. This is an advert on the building of the hotel.*

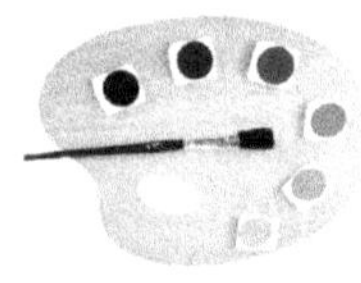

# 14

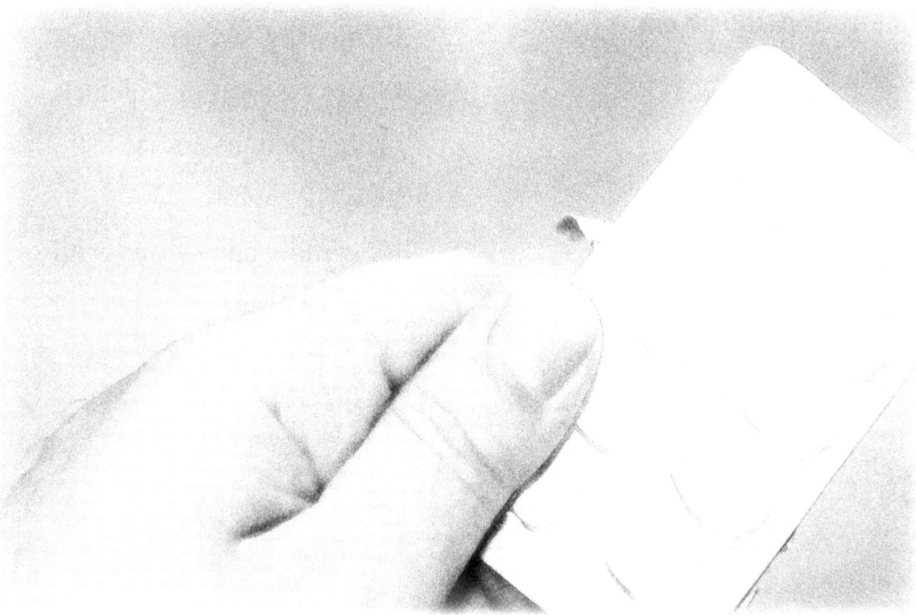

## **Aspirin**

*Aspirin*

## A

**Vokabeln**

1. die Apotheke - pharmacy
2. das Aspirin - aspirin
3. die Aufgabe - task
4. das Blatt - sheet (of paper)
5. die Chemie - chemistry
6. chemisch - chemical(adj)
   die Chemikalien - chemicals
7. dass - that (conj)
8. denken - to think
9. einige - some
10. (etwas) erhalten - to get (something),
    ankommen - to get (somewhere)
11. etwas - something
12. für - for
13. grau - grey
14. halb - half
15. sich hinsetzen - to sit down
16. intelligent - smart

17. der Junge - guy
18. das Klassenzimmer - classroom
19. das Kristal - crystal
20. die Lösung - solution, answer
21. nach - past;
    um halb neun - at half past eight
22. natürlich - of course
23. oft - often
24. das Papier - paper
25. die Pause - break, pause
26. die Prüfung - test
    prüfen - to test
    eine Prüfung bestehen - to pass a test
27. schließlich - at last
28. der Schreibtisch - desk
29. stinkend - stinking
30. das Studentenwohnheim - dorms
31. die Tablette - pill
32. die Uhr - watch
33. um eins - at one o'clock
34. versuchen - to try
35. weiß - white
36. wunderbar - wonderful
37. zehn - ten

## B

### Aspirin

Das ist ein Freund von Mike. Er heißt Alexander. Alexander kommt aus der Schweiz. Seine Muttersprache ist Französisch. Er spricht auch sehr gut Deutsch. Alexander wohnt im Studentenwohnheim. Alexander ist gerade in seinem Zimmer. Alexander hat heute eine Prüfung in Chemie. Er schaut auf die Uhr. Es ist acht Uhr. Es ist an der Zeit, zu gehen.

Alexander geht nach draußen. Er geht zur Universität. Die Uni ist in der Nähe des Wohnheims. Er braucht etwa zehn Minuten bis zur Uni. Alexander kommt zum Klassenzimmer. Er öffnet die Tür und schaut ins Klassenzimmer. Einige Studenten und der Lehrer sind da. Alexander betritt das Klassenzimmer.

„Hallo", sagt er.

„Hallo", antworten der Lehrer und die Studenten.

Alexander geht zu seinem Schreibtisch und setzt sich hin. Die Prüfung beginnt um halb neun. Der

### *Aspirin*

*This is Mike's friend. His name is Alexander. Alexander is from Switzerland. French is his native language. He can speak German very well too. Alexander lives in the dorms. Alexander is in his room now. Alexander has a chemistry test today. He looks at his watch. It is eight o'clock. It is time to go.*

*Alexander goes outside. He goes to the college. The college is near the dorms. It takes him about ten minutes to go to the college. Alexander comes to the chemical classroom. He opens the door and looks into the classroom. There are some students and the teacher there. Alexander comes into the classroom.*

*"Hello," he says.*

*"Hello," the teacher and the students answer.*

*Alexander comes to his desk and sits down. The chemistry test begins at half past eight.*

Lehrer kommt zu Alexanders Tisch.

„Hier ist deine Aufgabe“, sagt der Lehrer. Dann gibt er Alexander ein Blatt Papier mit der Aufgabe. „Du musst Aspirin herstellen. Du kannst von halb neun bis zwölf Uhr arbeiten. Fang bitte an“, sagt der Lehrer.

Alexander weiß, wie diese Aufgabe geht. Er nimmt einige Chemikalien und beginnt. Er arbeitet zehn Minuten lang. Schließlich erhält er etwas Graues und Stinkendes. Das ist nicht gutes Aspirin. Alexander weiß, dass er große, weiße Aspirinkristalle erhalten muss. Dann versucht er es wieder und wieder. Alexander arbeitet eine Stunde lang, aber das Ergebnis ist wieder grau und stinkend.

Alexander ist wütend und müde. Er kann es nicht verstehen. Er macht eine Pause und denkt ein bisschen nach. Alexander ist intelligent. Er denkt ein paar Minuten nach und findet dann die Lösung! Er steht auf.

„Kann ich zehn Minuten Pause machen?“, fragt er den Lehrer.

„Ja, natürlich“, antwortet der Lehrer.

Alexander geht nach draußen. Er findet eine Apotheke in der Nähe der Uni. Er geht hinein und kauft ein paar Tabletten Aspirin. Nach zehn Minuten kommt er zurück ins Klassenzimmer. Die Studenten sitzen da und arbeiten. Alexander setzt sich hin.

„Kann ich die Prüfung beenden?“, fragt Alexander den Lehrer nach fünf Minuten.

Der Lehrer kommt zu Alexanders Tisch. Er sieht große, weiße Aspirinkristalle. Der Lehrer ist überrascht. Er bleibt stehen und schaut eine Weile auf das Aspirin.

„Wunderbar! Dein Aspirin ist gut! Aber ich kann das nicht verstehen! Ich versuche oft, Aspirin herzustellen, aber alles, was ich herausbekomme, ist grau und stinkt“, sagt der Lehrer. „Du hast die Prüfung bestanden.“

*The teacher comes to Alexander's desk.*

*"Here is your task," the teacher says. Then he gives Alexander a sheet of paper with the task. "You must make aspirin. You can work from half past eight to twelve o'clock. Begin, please," the teacher says.*

*Alexander knows this task. He takes some chemicals and begins. He works for ten minutes. At last he gets something grey and stinking. This is not good aspirin. Alexander knows that he must get big white crystals of aspirin. Then he tries again and again. Alexander works for an hour but he gets something grey and stinking again.*

*Alexander is angry and tired. He cannot understand it. He stops and thinks a little. Alexander is a smart guy. He thinks for a minute and then finds the answer! He stands up.*

*"May I have a break for ten minutes?" Alexander asks the teacher.*

*"Of course, you may," the teacher answers.*

*Alexander goes outside. He finds a pharmacy near the college. He comes in and buys some pills of aspirin. In ten minutes he comes back to the classroom. The students sit and work. Alexander sits down.*

*"May I finish the test?" Alexander says to the teacher in five minutes.*

*The teacher comes to Alexander's desk. He sees big white crystals of aspirin. The teacher stops in surprise. He stands and looks at aspirin for a minute.*

*"It is wonderful! Your aspirin is so nice! But I cannot understand it! I often try to get aspirin and I get only something grey and stinking," the teacher says. "You passed the test," he says.*

Alexander geht nach der Prüfung weg. Der Lehrer sieht etwas Weißes auf Alexanders Tisch. Er geht zum Tisch und findet das Papier der Aspirintabletten.

*Alexander goes away after the test. The teacher sees something white at Alexander's desk. He comes to the desk and finds the paper from the aspirin pills.*

„Intelligenter Junge. Gut, Alexander, jetzt hast du ein Problem", sagt der Lehrer.

*"Smart guy. Ok, Alexander. Now you have a problem," the teacher says.*

# 15

## Anke und das Känguru

*Anke and the kangaroo*

## A

### Vokabeln

1. der Affe - monkey
2. ärgern - to bother
3. arm - poor
4. das Bücherregal - bookcase
5. der Eimer - pail
6. das Eis - ice-cream
7. fallen - to fall
   der Fall - fall
8. glücklich - happy
9. das Haar - hair
10. Hey! - Hey!
11. das Jahr- year
12. das Känguru - kangaroo
13. lass uns - let us
14. leise - quietly
15. der Löwe - lion
16. mich - me
17. nass - wet

18. Oh! - Oh!
19. das Ohr - ear
20. okay, gut - okay, well
21. der Plan - plan
    planen - to plan
22. die Puppe - doll
23. schlagen - to hit, to beat
24. der Schwanz - tail
25. sein - its (for neuter)
26. das Spielzeug - toy
27. stark - strong, strongly
28. studieren - to study
29. der Tiger - tiger
30. uns - us
31. voll - full
32. was - what
    Was ist das? - What is this?
    Welcher Tisch? - What table?
33. das Wasser - water
34. weinen, schreien, rufen - to cry
35. weit - wide, widely
36. wenn - when
37. das Zebra - zebra
38. ziehen - to pull
39. der Zoo - zoo
40. zusammen - together

## B

### Anke und das Känguru

Mike ist jetzt Student. Er studiert an der Universität. Er studiert Deutsch. Mike wohnt im Studentenwohnheim. Er ist Alexanders Nachbar.

Mike ist gerade in seinem Zimmer. Er nimmt sein Telefon und ruft seinen Freund Stefan an.

Stefan geht ans Telefon und sagt: „Hallo."

„Hallo Stefan. Ich bin es, Mike. Wie geht's dir?", sagt Mike.

„Hallo Mike. Mir geht's gut. Danke. Und dir?", antwortet Stefan.

„Mir geht's auch gut, danke. Ich werde einen Ausflug machen. Was hast du heute vor?", sagt Mike.

„Meine Schwester Anke will mit mir in den Zoo gehen. Ich werde jetzt mit ihr dorthin gehen. Lass uns zusammen gehen", sagt Stefan.

### *Anke and the kangaroo*

*Mike is a student now. He studies at a college. He studies German. Mike lives at the dorms. He lives next door to Alexander's.*

*Mike is in his room now. He takes the telephone and calls his friend Stefan.*

*"Hello," Stefan answers the call.*

*"Hello Stefan. It is Mike here. How are you?" Mike says.*

*"Hello Mike. I am fine. Thanks. And how are you?" Stefan answers.*

*"I am fine too. Thanks. I will go for a walk. What are your plans for today?" Mike says.*

*"My sister Anke asks me to take her to the zoo. I will take her there now. Let us go together," Stefan says.*

„Alles klar, ich komme mit. Wo treffen wir uns?“, fragt Mike.

*"Okay. I will go with you. Where will we meet?" Mike asks.*

„Lass uns an der Bushaltestelle Havenwelten treffen. Und frag Alexander, ob er auch mitkommen will“, sagt Stefan.

*"Let us meet at the bus stop Havenwelten. And ask Alexander to come with us too," Stefan says.*

„Alles klar. Tschüss“, antwortet Mike.

*"Okay. Bye," Mike answers.*

„Bis gleich“, sagt Stefan.

*"See you. Bye," Stefan says.*

Dann geht Mike zu Alexanders Zimmer. Alexander ist in seinem Zimmer.

*Then Mike goes to Alexander's room. Alexander is in his room.*

„Hallo“, sagt Mike.

*"Hello," Mike says.*

„Oh, hallo Mike. Komm rein“, sagt Alexander. Mike betritt das Zimmer.

*"Oh, hello Mike. Come in, please," Alexander says. Mike comes in.*

„Stefan, seine Schwester und ich gehen in den Zoo. Willst du mitkommen?“, fragt Mike.

*"Stefan, his sister and I will go to the zoo. Will you go together with us?" Mike asks.*

„Natürlich komme ich mit“, sagt Alexander.

*"Of course, I will go too!" Alexander says.*

Mike und Alexander fahren bis zur Bushaltestelle Havenwelten. Dort sehen sie Stefan und seine Schwester Anke.

*Mike and Alexander drive to the bus stop Havenwelten. They see Stefan and his sister Anke there.*

Stefans Schwester ist erst fünf. Sie ist ein kleines Mädchen und voller Energie. Sie mag Tiere sehr gerne. Aber Anke denkt, dass Tiere Spielzeug sind. Die Tiere rennen vor ihr weg, weil sie sie sehr ärgert. Sie zieht sie am Schwanz oder am Ohr, schlägt sie mit der Hand oder mit einem Spielzeug. Zuhause hat Anke einen Hund und eine Katze. Wenn Anke zuhause ist, sitzt der Hund unter dem Bett und die Katze auf dem Bücherregal. So kann Anke sie nicht kriegen.

*Stefan's sister is only five years old. She is a little girl and she is full of energy. She likes animals very much. But Anke thinks that animals are toys. The animals run away from her because she bothers them very much. She can pull tail or ear, hit with a hand or with a toy. Anke has a dog and a cat at home. When Anke is at home the dog is under a bed and the cat sits on the bookcase. So she cannot get them.*

Anke, Stefan, Mike und Alexander betreten den Zoo.

*Anke, Stefan, Mike and Alexander come into the zoo.*

Im Zoo gibt es sehr viele Tiere. Anke ist glücklich. Sie rennt zu den Löwen und Tigern. Sie schlägt das Zebra mit ihrer Puppe. Sie zieht so stark am Schwanz eines Affen, dass alle Affen schreiend wegrennen. Dann sieht Anke ein Känguru. Das Känguru trinkt Wasser aus einem Eimer. Anke lächelt und nähert sich dem Känguru langsam. Und dann...

*There are many animals in the zoo. Anke is very happy. She runs to the lion and to the tiger. She hits the zebra with her doll. She pulls the tail of a monkey so strong that all the monkeys run away crying. Then Anke sees a kangaroo. The kangaroo drinks water from a pail. Anke smiles and comes to the kangaroo very quietly. And then...*

„Hey!!! Kängruu-uu-uu!!“, schreit Anke und zieht

*"Hey!! Kangaroo-oo-oo!!" Anke cries and*

es am Schwanz. Das Känguru schaut Anke mit weit aufgerissenen Augen an. Vor Schreck macht es einen Satz, sodass der Wassereimer in die Luft fliegt und auf Anke fällt. Wasser läuft über ihr Haar, ihr Gesicht und ihr Kleid. Anke ist ganz nass.

„Du bist ein böses Känguru! Böse!“, ruft sie.

Einige Leute lächeln und einige Leute sagen: „Armes Mädchen.“ Stefan bringt Anke nach Hause.

„Du darfst die Tiere nicht ärgern“, sagt Stefan und gibt ihr ein Eis. Anke isst das Eis.

„Okay, ich werde nicht mehr mit sehr großen und wütenden Tieren spielen“, denkt Anke. “Ich werde nur noch mit kleinen Tieren spielen.“ Sie ist wieder glücklich.

*pulls its tail. The kangaroo looks at Anke with wide open eyes. It jumps in surprise so that the pail with water flies up and falls on Anke. Water runs down her hair, her face and her dress. Anke is all wet.*

*"You are a bad kangaroo! Bad!" she cries.*

*Some people smile and some people say: "Poor girl." Stefan takes Anke home.*

*"You must not bother the animals," Stefan says and gives an ice-cream to her. Anke eats the ice-cream.*

*"Okay. I will not play with very big and angry animals," Anke thinks. "I will play with little animals only." She is happy again.*

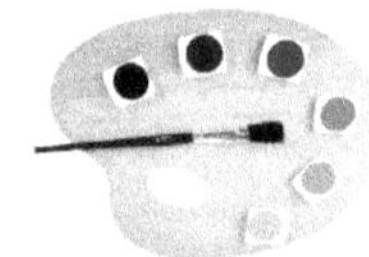

# 16

## Die Fallschirmspringer

*Parachutists*

# A

### Vokabeln

1. abgestürzt - fallen
2. anderer - other
3. sich anziehen - to put on
   angezogen - dressed
4. ausgestopft - stuffed; Fallschirmspringerpuppe - stuffed parachutist
5. aussteigen - to get off
6. das Dach - roof
7. eigen - own
8. einfach - just
9. fallend - falling
10. der Fallschirm - parachute
11. der Fallschirmspringer - parachutist
12. fangen - to catch
13. die Flugschau - airshow

14. das Flugzeug - airplane
15. gelb - yellow
16. glauben - to believe

    seinen Augen nicht trauen - to not believe one's eyes
17. der Gummi - rubber
18. die Hose - trousers
19. in - inside
20. die Jacke - jacket
21. die Kleidung - clothes
22. landen - to land
23. das Leben - life,

    Rettungstrick - life-saving trick
24. leise - silent, silently
25. die Luft - air
26. machen - to do
27. die Mannschaft - team
28. das Metall - metal
29. das Mitglied - member
30. nach - after
31. neun - nine
32. ob - if
33. Papa - daddy
34. der Pilot - pilot
35. das Publikum - audience
36. retten - to save
37. rot - red
38. schließen - to close
39. sein - to be
40. der Sitz - seat,

    sich hinsetzen - to take a seat
41. stoßen, ziehen - to push
42. super, toll - great
43. der Teil - part
44. trainieren - to train

    trainiert - trained
45. der Trick - trick
46. über - over
47. übrigens - by the way
48. der Verein - club
49. vorbereiten - to prepare
50. wirklich - real
51. wütend - angrily

## B

### Die Fallschirmspringer

Es ist Morgen. Mike kommt in Alexanders Zimmer. Alexander sitzt am Tisch und schreibt etwas. Alexanders Katze Minka sitzt auf Alexanders Bett. Sie schläft ruhig.

„Kann ich reinkommen?“, fragt Mike.

„Oh, Mike. Komm rein. Wie geht's dir?“,

### *Parachutists*

*It is morning. Mike comes to Alexander's room. Alexander is sitting at the table and writing something. Alexander's cat Minka is on Alexander's bed. It is sleeping quietly.*

*"May I come in?" Mike asks.*

*"Oh, Mike. Come in please. How are you?"*

antwortet Alexander.

*Alexander answers.*

„Gut, danke. Und dir?“, sagt Mike.

*"Fine. Thanks. How are you?" Mike says.*

„Danke, auch gut. Setz dich“, antwortet Alexander.

*"I am fine. Thanks. Sit down, please," Alexander answers.*

Mike setzt sich auf einen Stuhl.

*Mike sits on a chair.*

„Du weißt doch, dass ich Mitglied in einem Fallschirmspringerverein bin. Wir haben heute eine Flugschau“, sagt Mike. „Ich werde ein paar Sprünge machen.“

*"You know I am a member of a parachute club. We are having an airshow today," Mike says. "I am going to make some jumps there."*

„Das ist interessant“, antwortet Alexander. „Ich komme vielleicht zuschauen.“

*"It is very interesting," Alexander answers. "I may come to see the airshow."*

„Wenn du willst, kann ich dich mitnehmen und du kannst in einem Flugzeug mitfliegen“, sagt Mike.

*"If you want I can take you there and you can fly in an airplane," Mike says.*

„Echt? Das wäre super!“, ruft Alexander. „Um wie viel Uhr ist die Flugschau?“

*"Really? That will be great!" Alexander cries. "What time is the airshow?"*

„Sie fängt um zehn Uhr morgens an“, antwortet Mike. „Stefan kommt auch. Übrigens, wir brauchen Hilfe, eine Fallschirmspringerpuppe aus dem Flugzeug zu werfen. Kannst du helfen?“

*"It begins at ten o'clock in the morning," Mike answers. "Stefan will come too. By the way we need help to push a stuffed parachutist out of the airplane. Will you help?"*

„Eine Fallschirmspringerpuppe? Warum?“, fragt Alexander überrascht.

*"A stuffed parachutist? Why?" Alexander says in surprise.*

„Ach, weißt du, das ist ein Teil der Schau“, sagt Mike. „Es ist ein Rettungstrick. Die Puppe fällt herunter. In dem Moment fliegt ein echter Fallschirmspringer zu ihr, fängt sie und öffnet seinen eigenen Fallschirm. Der ‚Mann‘ ist gerettet!“

*"You see, it is a part of the show," Mike says. "This is a life-saving trick. The stuffed parachutist falls down. At this time a real parachutist flies to it, catches it and opens his own parachute. The 'man' is saved!"*

„Toll!“, antwortet Alexander. „Ich helfe. Lass uns gehen!“

*"Great!" Alexander answers. "I will help. Let's go!"*

Alexander und Mike gehen nach draußen. Sie kommen zur Bushaltestelle Freigebiet und nehmen einen Bus. Es dauert nur zehn Minuten bis zur Flugschau. Als sie aus dem Bus steigen, sehen sie Stefan.

*Alexander and Mike go outside. They come to the bus stop Freigebiet and take a bus. It takes only ten minutes to go to the airshow. When they get off the bus, they see Stefan.*

„Hallo Stefan“, sagt Mike. „Lass uns zum Flugzeug gehen.“

*"Hello Stefan," Mike says. "Let's go to the airplane."*

Beim Flugzeug sehen sie eine Fallschirmspringermannschaft. Der Führer der

*They see a parachute team at the airplane. They come to the head of the team. The head of the team is dressed in red trousers and a*

Mannschaft hat eine rote Hose und eine rote Jacke an.

*red jacket.*

„Hallo Martin“, sagt Mike. „Alexander und Stefan helfen beim Rettungstrick.“

*"Hello Martin," Mike says. "Alexander and Stefan will help with the life-saving trick."*

„Okay. Hier ist die Puppe“, sagt Martin. Er gibt ihnen die Fallschirmspringerpuppe. Die Puppe trägt eine rote Hose und eine rote Jacke.

*"Okay. The stuffed parachutist is here," Martin says. He gives them the stuffed parachutist. The stuffed parachutist is dressed in red trousers and a red jacket.*

„Sie trägt die gleiche Kleidung wie du“, sagt Stefan und grinst Martin an.

*"It is dressed like you," Stefan says smiling to Martin.*

„Wir haben keine Zeit, darüber zu reden“, sagt Martin. „Nehmt sie mit in dieses Flugzeug.“

*"We have no time to talk about it," Martin says. "Take it into this airplane."*

Alexander und Stefan bringen die Puppe ins Flugzeug. Sie setzen sich neben den Piloten. Die ganze Fallschirmspringermannschaft außer ihrem Führer besteigt das Flugzeug. Sie schließen die Tür. Nach fünf Minuten ist das Flugzeug in der Luft. Als es über Bremerhaven fliegt, sieht Stefan sein Haus.

*Alexander and Stefan take the stuffed parachutist into the airplane. They take seats at the pilot. All the parachute team but its head gets into the airplane. They close the door. In five minutes the airplane is in the air. When it flies over Bremerhaven Stefan sees his own house.*

„Schau! Da ist mein Haus!“, ruft Stefan.

*"Look! My house is there!" Stefan cries.*

Alexander schaut aus dem Fenster auf Straßen, Plätze und Parks. Es ist toll, in einem Flugzeug zu fliegen.

*Alexander looks through the window at streets, squares, and parks of the city. It is wonderful to fly in an airplane.*

„Zum Sprung bereit machen!“, ruft der Pilot. Die Fallschirmspringer stehen auf. Sie öffnen die Tür.

*"Prepare to jump!" the pilot cries. The parachutists stand up. They open the door.*

„Zehn, neun, acht, sieben, sechs, fünf, vier, drei, zwei, eins! Los!“, ruft der Pilot.

*"Ten, nine, eight, seven, six, five, four, three, two, one. Go!" the pilot cries.*

Die Fallschirmspringer beginnen, aus dem Flugzeug zu springen. Das Publikum auf dem Boden sieht rote, grüne, weiße, blaue und gelbe Fallschirme. Es sieht sehr schön aus. Martin, der Führer der Mannschaft, schaut auch nach oben. Die Fallschirmspringer fliegen nach unten und einige landen bereits.

*The parachutists begin to jump out of the airplane. The audience down on the land sees red, green, white, blue, yellow parachutes. It looks very nice. Martin, the head of the parachute team is looking up too. The parachutists are flying down and some are landing already.*

„Okay, gute Arbeit, Jungs“, sagt Martin und geht in ein Café in der Nähe, um Kaffee zu trinken.

*"Okay. Good work guys," Martin says and goes to the nearby café to drink some coffee.*

Die Flugschau geht weiter.

*The airshow goes on.*

„Für den Rettungstrick bereit machen!“, ruft der Pilot. Stefan und Alexander bringen die Puppe

*"Prepare for the life-saving trick!" the pilot cries. Stefan and Alexander take the stuffed*

zur Tür.

*parachutist to the door.*

„Zehn, neun, acht, sieben, sechs, fünf, vier, drei, zwei, eins! Los!“, ruft der Pilot.

*"Ten, nine, eight, seven, six, five, four, three, two, one. Go!" the pilot cries.*

Alexander und Stefan stoßen die Puppe aus der Tür. Sie fällt heraus, bleibt dann aber hängen. Ihre Gummihand ist an einem Metallteil des Flugzeugs hängengeblieben.

*Alexander and Stefan push the stuffed parachutist through the door. It goes out but then stops. Its rubber "hand" catches on some metal part of the airplane.*

„Los, auf, Jungs!“, ruft der Pilot.

*"Go-go boys!" the pilot cries.*

Die Jungs ziehen mit aller Kraft an der Puppe, aber sie bekommen sie nicht los.

*The boys push the stuffed parachutist very strongly but cannot get it out.*

Das Publikum unten auf dem Boden sieht einen Mann in Rot gekleidet in der Flugzeugtür. Zwei andere Männer versuchen, ihn herauszustoßen. Die Leute trauen ihren Augen nicht. Es dauert etwa eine Minute. Dann fällt der Fallschirmspringer in Rot nach unten. Ein anderer Fallschirmspringer springt aus dem Flugzeug und versucht, ihn zu fangen. Aber er schafft es nicht. Der Fallschirmspringer in Rot fällt weiter. Er fällt durch das Dach in das Café. Das Publikum schaut schweigend zu. Dann sehen die Leute einen in rot gekleideten Mann aus dem Café rennen. Der Mann in Rot ist Martin, der Führer der Fallschirmspinger-mannschaft. Aber das Publikum denkt, dass er der abgestürzte Fallschirmspringer ist. Er schaut nach oben und ruft wütend: „Wenn ihr einen Mann nicht fangen könnt, dann versucht es nicht!“

*The audience down on the land sees a man dressed in red in the airplane door. Two other men are trying to push him out. People cannot believe their eyes. It goes on about a minute. Then the parachutist in red falls down. Another parachutist jumps out of the airplane and tries to catch it. But he cannot do it. The parachutist in red falls down. It falls through the roof inside of the café. The audience looks silently. Then the people see a man dressed in red run outside of the café. This man in red is Martin, the head of the parachutist team. But the audience thinks that he is that falling parachutist. He looks up and cries angrily. "If you cannot catch a man then do not try it!"*

Das Publikum ist still.

*The audience is silent.*

„Papa, dieser Mann ist sehr stark“, sagt ein kleines Mädchen zu ihrem Vater.

*"Daddy, this man is very strong," a little girl says to her dad.*

„Er ist gut trainiert“, antwortet der Vater.

*"He is well trained," the dad answers.*

Nach der Flugschau gehen Stefan und Alexander zu Mike.

*After the airshow Alexander and Stefan go to Mike.*

„Wie war unsere Arbeit?“, fragt Stefan.

*"How is our work?" Stefan asks.*

„Ähm...Oh, sehr gut. Danke“, antwortet Mike.

*"Ah... Oh, it is very good. Thank you," Mike answers.*

„Wenn du Hilfe brauchst, sag es einfach“, sagt Alexander.

*"If you need some help just say," Alexander says.*

# 17

## Mach das Gas aus!

*Turn the gas off!*

## A

### Vokabeln

1. alles - everything
2. der Bahnhof - railway station
3. befehlen - to order
4. blass - pale
5. das Butterbrot - sandwich
6. deswegen - so
7. drehen - to turn;
   anmachen - to turn on;
   ausmachen - to turn off
8. elf - eleven
9. erstarren - to freeze
10. die Fahrkarte - ticket
11. das Feuer - fire
12. fremd - strange
13. füllen - to fill up
14. das Gas - gas
15. das Gefühl - feeling
16. der Kessel - kettle
17. der Kilometer - kilometer

18. der Kindergarten - kindergarten
19. klingeln - to ring,
das Klingeln - ring
20. die Miezekatze - pussycat
21. der Moment - moment
22. plötzlich - suddenly
23. sagen - to tell, to say
24. schlau - sly, slyly
25. schnell - quick, quickly
26. die Sekretärin - secretary
27. sofort - immediately
28. sorgfältig - careful
29. die Stimme - voice
30. der Telefonhörer - phone handset
31. übergreifen - to spread
32. vergessen - forget
33. vierundvierzig - forty-four
34. warm - warm;
aufwärmen - to warm up
35. der Wasserhahn - tap
36. wer - who
37. werden - will
38. wohnhaft - living
39. der Zug - train
40. in der Zwischenzeit - meanwhile
41. zwanzig - twenty

## B

**Mach das Gas aus!**

Es ist sieben Uhr morgens. Stefan und Anke schlafen. Ihre Mutter ist in der Küche. Die Mutter heißt Linda. Linda ist vierundvierzig. Sie ist eine sorgfältige Frau. Linda putzt die Küche, bevor sie zur Arbeit geht. Sie ist Sekretärin. Sie arbeitet zwanzig Kilometer außerhalb von Bremerhaven. Linda fährt normalerweise mit dem Zug zur Arbeit.

Sie geht nach draußen. Der Bahnhof ist in der Nähe, deswegen geht Linda zu Fuß dorthin. Sie kauft eine Fahrkarte und steigt ein. Es dauert etwa zwanzig Minuten bis zu ihrer Arbeit. Linda sitzt im Zug und schaut aus dem Fenster.

Plötzlich erstarrt sie. Der Kessel! Er steht auf dem Herd und sie hat vergessen, das Gas auszumachen. Stefan und Anke schlafen. Das Feuer kann auf die Möbel übergreifen und dann... Linda wird blass. Aber sie ist eine intelligente Frau und kurz darauf weiß sie, was

***Turn the gas off!***

*It is seven o'clock in the morning. Stefan and María are sleeping. Their mother is in the kitchen. The mother's name is Linda. Linda is forty-four years old. She is a careful woman. Linda cleans the kitchen before she goes to work. She is a secretary. She works twenty kilometers away from Bremerhaven. Linda usually goes to work by train.*

*She goes outside. The railway station is nearby, so Linda goes there on foot. She buys a ticket and gets on a train. It takes about twenty minutes to go to work. Linda sits in the train and looks out of the window.*

*Suddenly she freezes. The kettle! It is standing on the cooker and she forgot to turn the gas off! Stefan and Anke are sleeping. The fire can spread on the furniture and then... Linda turns pale. But she is a smart woman and in a minute she knows*

zu tun ist. Sie bittet eine Frau und einen Mann, die neben ihr sitzen, bei ihr zu Hause anzurufen und Stefan über den Kessel zu informieren.

*what to do. She asks a woman and a man, who sit nearby, to telephone her home and tell Stefan about the kettle.*

In der Zwischenzeit steht Stefan auf, wäscht sich und geht in die Küche. Er nimmt den Kessel vom Tisch, füllt ihn mit Wasser und stellt ihn auf den Herd. Dann nimmt er Brot und Butter und macht Butterbrote. Anke kommt in die Küche.

*Meanwhile Stefan gets up, washes and goes to the kitchen. He takes the kettle off the table, fills it up with water and puts it on the cooker. Then he takes bread and butter and makes sandwiches. Anke comes into the kitchen.*

„Wo ist meine kleine Miezekatze?“, fragt sie.

*"Where is my little pussycat?" she asks.*

„Ich weiß es nicht“, antworte Stefan. „Geh ins Bad und wasch dein Gesicht. Wir trinken jetzt Tee und essen Brote. Dann bring ich dich in den Kindergarten.“

*"I do not know," Stefan answers. "Go to the bathroom and wash your face. We will drink some tea and eat some sandwiches now. Then I will take you to the kindergarten."*

Anke will sich nicht waschen. „Ich kann den Wasserhahn nicht anmachen“, sagt sie schlau.

*Anke does not want to wash. "I cannot turn on the water tap," she says slyly.*

„Ich helfe dir“, sagt ihr Bruder. In diesem Moment klingelt das Telefon. Anke rennt schnell zum Telefon und nimmt den Hörer ab.

*"I will help you," her brother says. At this moment the telephone rings. Anke runs quickly to the telephone and takes the handset.*

„Hallo, hier ist der Zoo. Und wer ist da?“, sagt sie. Stefan nimmt ihr den Hörer weg und sagt: „Hallo, Stefan hier.“

*"Hello, this is the zoo. And who are you?" she says. Stefan takes the handset from her and says. "Hello. This is Stefan."*

„Bist du Stefan Müller, wohnhaft in der Nelkenstraße elf?“, fragt die Stimme einer fremden Frau.

*"Are you Stefan Müller living at Nelkenstraße eleven?" the voice of a strange woman asks.*

„Ja“, antwortet Stefan.

*"Yes," Stefan answers.*

„Geh sofort in die Küche und mach das Gas aus“, ruft die Stimme der Frau.

*"Go to the kitchen immediately and turn the gas off!" the woman's voice cries.*

„Wer sind Sie? Warum soll ich das Gas ausmachen?“, fragt Stefan überrascht.

*"Who are you? Why must I turn the gas off?" Stefan says in surprise.*

„Mach es jetzt!“, befielt die Stimme.

*"Do it now!" the voice orders.*

Stefan macht das Gas aus. Anke und Stefan schauen verwundert auf den Kessel.

*Stefan turns the gas off. Anke and Stefan look at the kettle in surprise.*

„Ich verstehe das nicht“, sagt Stefan. „Woher weiß diese Frau, dass wir Tee trinken wollten?“

*"I do not understand," Stefan says. "How can this woman know that we will drink tea?"*

„Ich habe Hunger“, sagt seine Schwester. „Wann essen wir?“

*"I am hungry," his sister says. "When will we eat?"*

„Ich habe auch Hunger“, sagt Stefan und macht

das Gas wieder an. In diesem Moment klingelt das Telefon wieder.

„Hallo“, sagt Stefan.

„Bist du Stefan Müller, wohnhaft in der Nelkenstraße elf?“, fragt die Stimme eines fremden Mannes.

„Ja“, antwortet Stefan.

„Mach sofort das Gas aus! Sei vorsichtig!“, befiehlt die Stimme.

„Okay“, sagt Stefan und macht das Gas wieder aus.

„Lass uns in den Kindergarten gehen“, sagt Stefan zu Anke in dem Gefühl, dass sie heute keinen Tee trinken werden.

„Nein. Ich will Tee und Brot mit Butter“, sagt Anke wütend.

„Gut, lass uns versuchen, den Kessel wieder zu wärmen“, sagt ihr Bruder und stellt das Gas an.

Das Telefon klingelt und dieses Mal befiehlt ihre Mutter, das Gas abzustellen. Dann erklärt sie alles. Endlich trinken Anke und Stefan Tee und gehen in den Kindergarten.

*"I am hungry too," Stefan says and turns the gas on again. At this minute the telephone rings again.*

*"Hello," Stefan says.*

*"Are you Stefan Müller who lives at Nelkenstraße eleven?" the voice of a strange man asks.*

*"Yes," Stefan answers.*

*"Turn off the cooker gas immediately! Be careful!" the voice orders.*

*"Okay," Stefan says and turns the gas off again.*

*"Let's go to the kindergarten," Stefan says to Anke feeling that they will not drink tea today.*

*"No. I want some tea and bread with butter," Anke says angrily.*

*"Well, let's try to warm up the kettle again," her brother says and turns the gas on.*

*The telephone rings and this time their mother orders to turn the gas off. Then she explains everything. At last Anke and Stefan drink tea and go to the kindergarten.*

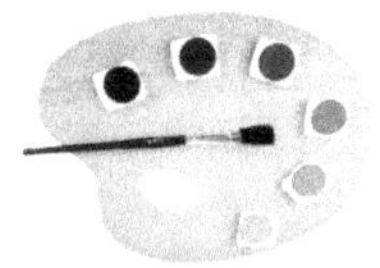

# 18

## Eine Arbeitsvermittlung

*A job agency*

### A

**Vokabeln**

1. der Arm - arm
2. auch - also
3. beraten - to consult
4. der Berater - consultant
5. der Boden - floor
6. da, wie - as
7. einverstanden sein - to agree
8. einzeln - individually
9. elektrisch - electric
10. empfehlen - to recommend
11. die Erfahrung - experience
12. ernst - seriously
13. führen - running
14. fünfzehn - fifteen
15. die Geschichte - story

16. der/die/das gleiche - the same
gleichzeitig - at the same time
17. grauhaarig - grey-headed
18. halb - half
19. die Handarbeit - manual work
20. der Helfer - helper
21. das Kabel - cable
22. die Kopfarbeit - mental work
23. sechzig - sixty
24. sich kennen - to know each other
25. klar, sicher - sure
26. lassen - to let
27. die Matratze - mattress
28. die Nummer - number
29. die Position - position
30. sich Sorgen machen - to worry
Mach dir keinen Kopf! - Do not worry!
31. die Stadt - town
32. pro Stunde - per hour
33. stark - strong, strongly
34. der Strom - current
35. tödlich - deadly
36. der Verlag - publishing
37. verwirrt - confused
38. vielseitig, alles könnend - all-round
39. vorsichtig - carefully
genau zuhören - to listen carefully
40. war - was
41. zittern - to shake

## B

### Eine Arbeitsvermittlung

Eines Tages kommt Alexander in Mikes Zimmer und sieht seinen Freund zitternd auf dem Bett liegen. Alexander sieht einige Stromkabel, die von Mike zum Wasserkocher führen. Alexander glaubt, dass Mike einen tödlichen Stromschlag abbekommen hat. Er geht schnell zum Bett, nimmt die Matratze und zieht stark daran. Mike fällt auf den Boden. Dann steht er auf und sieht Alexander verwundert an.

„Was war das denn?“, fragt Mike.

„Du standest unter Strom“, sagt Alexander.

„Nein, ich habe Musik gehört“, sagt Mike und zeigt auf seinen CD-Spieler.

„Oh, Entschuldigung“, sagt Alexander. Er ist verwirrt.

### *A job agency*

*One day Alexander goes to Mike's room and sees that his friend is lying on the bed shaking. Alexander sees some electrical cables running from Mike to the electric kettle. Alexander believes that Mike is under a deadly electric current. He quickly goes to the bed, takes the mattress and pulls it strongly. Mike falls to the floor. Then he stands up and looks at Alexander in surprise.*

*"What was it?" Mike asks.*

*"You were on electrical current," Alexander says.*

*"No, I was listening to the music," Mike says and shows his CD player.*

*"Oh, I am sorry," Alexander says. He is*

„Schon gut, mach dir keinen Kopf", sagt Mike ruhig und macht seine Hose sauber.

„Stefan und ich gehen zu einer Arbeitsvermittlung. Willst du mitkommen?", fragt Alexander.

„Klar, lass uns zusammen gehen", sagt Mike.

Sie gehen nach draußen und nehmen den Bus Nummer 7. Sie brauchen etwa fünfzehn Minuten bis zur Arbeitsvermittlung. Stefan ist schon dort. Sie betreten das Gebäude. Vor dem Büro der Arbeitsvermittlung ist eine lange Schlange. Sie stellen sich an. Nach einer halben Stunde betreten sie das Büro. Im Zimmer sind ein Stuhl und ein paar Bücherregale. Am Tisch sitzt ein grauhaariger Mann. Er ist etwa sechzig.

„Kommt rein, Jungs", sagt er freundlich. „Setzt euch, bitte."

Stefan, Mike und Alexander setzen sich.

„Ich bin Georg Profit. Ich bin Arbeitsberater. Normalerweise spreche ich einzeln mit Besuchern. Aber da ihr alle Studenten seid und euch kennt, kann ich euch zusammen beraten. Seid ihr einverstanden?"

„Ja", sagt Stefan. „Wir haben drei, vier Stunden frei pro Tag. Wir brauchen für diese Zeit einen Job."

„Gut, ich habe ein paar Jobs für Studenten. Und du, mach deinen CD-Spieler aus", sagt Herr Profit zu Mike.

„Ich kann gleichzeitig Ihnen zuhören und Musik hören", sagt Mike.

„Wenn du ernsthaft einen Job willst, mach die Musik aus und hör mir genau zu", sagt Herr Profit. „Also, was für einen Job wollt ihr denn. Wollt ihr Hand- oder Kopfarbeit?

„Ich kann jede Arbeit machen", sagt Alexander. „Ich bin stark. Wollen Sie es testen?", fragt er und stützt seinen Arm auf Herrn Profits Tisch auf.

*confused.*

*"It's okay. Do not worry," Mike answers quietly cleaning his trousers.*

*"Stefan and I go to a job agency. Do you want to go with us?" Alexander asks.*

*"Sure. Let's go together," Mike says.*

*They go outside and take the bus number seven. It takes them about fifteen minutes to go to the job agency. Stefan is already there. They come into the building. There is a long queue to the office of the job agency. They stand in the queue. In half an hour they come into the office. There is a table and some bookcases in the room. A gray-headed man is sitting at the table. He is about sixty years old.*

*"Come in guys!" he says friendly. "Take seats, please."*

*Stefan, Mike and Alexander sit down.*

*"My name is Georg Profit. I am a job consultant. Usually I speak with visitors individually. But as you are all students and know each other I can consult you all together. Do you agree?"*

*"Yes, sir," Stefan says. "We have three or four hours of free time every day. We need to find jobs for that time, sir."*

*"Well. I have some jobs for students. And you take off your player," Mr. Profit says to Mike.*

*"I can listen to you and to music at the same time," Mike says.*

*"If you seriously want to get a job take the player off and listen carefully to what I say," Mr. Profit says. "Now guys say what kind of job do you need? Do you need mental or manual work?"*

*"I can do any work," Alexander says. "I am strong. Want to arm?" he says and puts his arm on Mr. Profit's table.*

„Das hier ist kein Sportverein, aber wenn du willst..." sagt Herr Profit. Er stützt seinen Arm auf den Tisch auf und drückt Alexanders Arm schnell nach unten. „Wie du siehst, musst du nicht nur stark, sondern auch schlau sein."

„Ich kann auch Denkarbeit machen", sagt Alexander. Er will unbedingt einen Job. „Ich kann Geschichten schreiben. Ich habe ein paar Geschichten über meine Heimatstadt."

„Das ist sehr interessant", sagt Herr Profit. Er greift nach einem Blatt Papier. „Der Verlag ‚All-Round' braucht einen jungen Helfer als Schreiber. Sie zahlen neun Euro pro Stunde."

„Super", sagt Alexander. „Kann ich das versuchen?"

„Natürlich. Hier sind Telefonnummer und Adresse", sagt Herr Profit und gibt Alexander ein Blatt Papier.

„Und ihr Jungs könnt zwischen einem Job auf einem Bauernhof, in einer Computerfirma, bei einer Zeitung oder im Supermarkt wählen. Da ihr keine Erfahrung habt, empfehle ich euch, mit der Arbeit auf dem Bauernhof anzufangen. Sie brauchen zwei Arbeiter", sagt Herr Profit zu Stefan und Mike.

„Wie viel zahlen sie?", fragt Stefan.

„Mal schaun...", Herr Profit schaut auf den Computer. „Sie brauchen Arbeiter für drei oder vier Stunden am Tag und zahlen sieben Euro pro Stunde. Samstag und Sonntag sind frei. Seid ihr einverstanden?", fragt er.

„Ja, bin ich", sagt Stefan.

„Ich auch", sagt Mike.

„Gut, nehmt die Telefonnummer und die Adresse des Bauernhofs", sagt Herr Profit und gibt ihnen eine Blatt Papier.

„Dankeschön, Herr Profit", sagen die Jungs und gehen nach draußen.

*"It is not a sport club here but if you want..." Mr. Profit says. He puts his arm on the table and quickly pushes down Alexander's arm. "As you see son, you must be not only strong but also smart."*

*"I can work mentally too, sir," Alexander says again. He wants to get a job very much. "I can write stories. I have some stories about my native town."*

*"This is very interesting," Mr. Profit says. He takes a sheet of paper. "The publishing house "All-round" needs a young helper for a writing position. They pay nine euro per hour."*

*"Cool!" Alexander says. "Can I try?"*

*"Sure. Here are their telephone number and their address," Mr. Profit says and gives a sheet of paper to Alexander.*

*"And you guys can choose a job on a farm, in a computer firm, on a newspaper or in a supermarket. As you do not have any experience I recommend you to begin to work in a farm. They need two workers," Mr. Profit says to Stefan and Mike.*

*"How much do they pay?" Stefan asks.*

*"Let me see..." Mr. Profit looks into the computer. "They need workers for three or four hours a day and they pay seven euros per hour. Saturdays and Sundays are free. Do you agree?" he asks.*

*"I agree," Stefan says.*

*"I agree too," Mike says.*

*"Well. Take the telephone number and the address of the farm," Mr. Profit says and gives a sheet of paper to them.*

*"Thank you, sir," the boys say and go outside.*

# 19

## Stefan und Mike waschen den Laster (Teil 1)

*Stefan and Mike wash the truck (part 1)*

## A

### Vokabeln

1. abladen - to unload
2. achter - eighth
3. anfangen - to start
4. ankommen - to arrive
5. der Arbeitgeber - employer
6. benutzen - to use
7. der Besitzer - owner
8. die Bremse - brake,
   bremsen - to brake
9. dritter - third
10. entlang - along
11. erst - at first
12. das Feld - field
13. der Führerschein - driving license
14. fünfter - fifth

15. größer - bigger
16. der Hof - yard
17. die Kiste - box
18. kontrollieren - to check
19. die Küste - seashore
20. laden - to load
21. langsam - slowly
22. die Maschine - machine
23. das Meer - sea
24. der Meter - meter
25. der Motor - engine
26. nahe - close
27. näher - closer
28. neunter - ninth
29. passend - suitable
30. das Rad- wheel
31. das Saatgut - seed
32. sauber machen, putzen - to clean
33. schaukeln - to pitch
34. das Schiff - ship
35. sechster - sixth
36. siebter - seventh
37. die Stärke- strength
38. die Straße - road
39. treiben - to float
40. treten - to step
41. viel - lot
42. vierte - fourth
43. vorne - front
    die Vorderräder - front wheels
44. warten - to wait
45. waschen, putzen - to wash
46. weit - far
47. weiter - further
48. die Welle - wave
49. zehnter - tenth
50. ziemlich - quite
51. zweiter - second

 B

### Stefan und Mike waschen den Laster (Teil 1)

Stefan und Mike arbeiten jetzt auf einem Bauernhof. Sie arbeiten drei, vier Stunden am Tag. Die Arbeit ist ziemlich schwer. Sie müssen jeden Tag viel arbeiten. Sie machen den Hof jeden zweiten Tag sauber. Sie putzen die Maschinen jeden dritten Tag. Jeden vierten Tag arbeiten sie auf den Feldern.

Ihr Arbeitgeber heißt Uwe Schmidt. Herr

### *Stefan and Mike wash the truck (part 1)*

*Stefan and Mike are working on a farm now. They work three or four hours every day. The work is quite hard. They must do a lot of work every day. They clean the farm yard every second day. They wash the farm machines every third day. Every fourth day they work in the farm fields.*

*Their employer's name is Uwe Schmidt. Mr.*

Schmidt ist der Besitzer des Bauernhofs und er macht die meiste Arbeit. Herr Schmidt arbeitet sehr hart. Er gibt Stefan und Mike auch viel Arbeit.

*Schmidt is the owner of the farm and he does most of the work. Mr. Schmidt works very hard. He also gives a lot of work to Stefan and Mike.*

„Hey Jungs, macht die Maschinen fertig sauber und fahrt dann mit dem Laster zur Transportfirma Rapid“, sagt Herr Schmidt. „Sie haben eine Ladung für mich. Ladet die Kisten mit dem Saatgut auf den Laster, bringt sie zum Bauernhof und ladet sie auf dem Hof ab. Beeilt euch, denn ich brauche das Saatgut heute. Und vergesst nicht, den Laster zu waschen.“

*"Hey boys, finish cleaning the machines, take the truck and go to the transport firm Rapid," Mr. Schmidt says. "They have a load for me. Load boxes with the seed in the truck, bring them to the farm, and unload in the farm yard. Do it quickly because I need to use the seed today. And do not forget to wash the truck."*

„Okay“, sagt Stefan. Sie machen die Maschine fertig sauber und steigen in den Laster. Stefan hat einen Führerschein, deswegen fährt er. Er macht den Motor an, fährt erst langsam durch den Hof und dann schnell die Straße entlang. Die Transportfirma Rapid ist nicht weit vom Bauernhof. Sie kommen dort nach fünfzehn Minuten an. Dort suchen sie die Verladetür Nummer zehn.

*"Okay," Stefan says. They finish cleaning and get into the truck. Stefan has a driving license so he drives the truck. He starts the engine and drives at first slowly through the farm yard, then quickly along the road. The transport firm Rapid is not far from the farm. They arrive there in fifteen minutes. They look for the loading door number ten there.*

Stefan fährt den Laster vorsichtig über den Hof. Sie fahren an der ersten Verladetür vorbei, an der zweiten, an der dritten, an der vierten, an der fünften, an der sechsten, an der siebten, an der achten und dann an der neunten. Stefan fährt zur zehnten Verladetür und hält an.

*Stefan drives the truck carefully through the loading yard. They go past the first loading door, past the second loading door, past the third, past the fourth, past the fifth, past the sixth, past the seventh, past the eighth, then past the ninth loading door. Stefan drives to the tenth loading door and stops.*

„Wir müssen erst die Ladeliste kontrollieren“, sagt Mike, der schon Erfahrung mit den Ladelisten in dieser Firma hat. Er geht zum Verlader, der an der Tür arbeitet, und gibt ihm die Ladeliste. Der Verlader lädt schnell fünf Kisten in ihren Laster. Mike kontrolliert die Kisten sorgfältig. Alle Kisten haben Nummern von der Ladeliste.

*"We must check the loading list first," Mike says who already has some experience with loading lists at this transport firm. He goes to the loader who works at the door and gives him the loading list. The loader loads quickly five boxes into their truck. Mike checks the boxes carefully. All numbers on the boxes have numbers from the loading list.*

„Die Nummern stimmen. Wir können jetzt gehen“, sagt Mike.

*"Numbers are correct. We can go now," Mike says.*

„Okay“, sagt Stefan und macht den Motor an. „Ich denke, wir können jetzt den Laster waschen. Nicht weit von hier ist ein passender Ort.“

*"Okay," Stefan says and starts the engine, "I think we can wash the truck now. There is a suitable place not far from here."*

Nach fünf Minuten kommen sie an die Küste.

*In five minutes they arrive to the seashore.*

„Willst du den Laster hier waschen?“, fragt Mike überrascht.

*"Do you want to wash the truck here?" Mike asks in surprise.*

„Ja! Schöner Platz, nicht?“, sagt Stefan.

*"Yeah! It is a nice place, isn't it?" Stefan says.*

„Und woher bekommen wir einen Eimer?“, fragt Mike.

*"And where will we take a pail?" Mike asks.*

„Wir brauchen keinen Eimer. Ich fahre ganz nah ans Meer. Wir nehmen das Wasser aus dem Meer“, sagt Stefan und fährt ganz nah ans Wasser. Die Vorderräder stehen im Wasser und die Wellen umspülen sie.

*"We do not need any pail. I will drive very close to the sea. We will take the water from the sea," Stefan says and drives very close to the water. The front wheels go in the water and the waves run over them.*

„Lass uns aussteigen und anfangen, zu waschen“, sagt Mike.

*"Let's get out and begin washing," Mike says.*

„Warte kurz, ich fahre noch etwas näher ran“, sagt Stefan und fährt ein, zwei Meter weiter. „So ist es besser.“

*"Wait a minute. I will drive a bit closer," Stefan says and drives one or two meters further. "It is better now."*

Da kommt eine größere Welle und das Wasser hebt den Laster ein bisschen nach oben und trägt ihn langsam weiter ins Meer.

*Then a bigger wave comes and the water lifts the truck a little and carries it slowly further into the sea.*

„Stopp! Stefan, halte den Laster an!“, ruft Mike. „Wir sind schon im Wasser! Bitte, halt an!“

*"Stop! Stefan, stop the truck!" Mike cries. "We are in the water already! Please, stop!"*

„Er hält nicht an!“, ruft Stefan und tritt mit aller Kraft die Bremse. „Ich kann ihn nicht anhalten.“

*"It will not stop!!" Stefan cries stepping on the brake with all his strength. "I cannot stop it!!"*

Der Laster treibt langsam weiter aufs Meer und schaukelt auf den Wellen wie ein kleines Schiff.

*The truck is slowly floating further in the sea pitching on the waves like a little ship.*

(Fortsetzung folgt)

*(to be continued)*

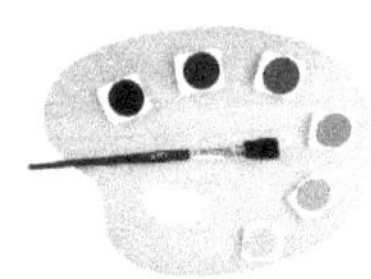

# 20

## Stefan und Mike waschen den Laster (Teil 2)

*Stefan and Mike wash the truck (part2)*

## A

**Vokabeln**

1. das Beispiel - example;
   zum Beispiel - for example
2. beständig - constant
3. die Feier - ceremony
4. feuern - to fire
5. der Fluss - flow
6. fotografieren - to photograph;
   der Fotograf - photographer
7. freisetzen - to set free
8. fünfundzwanzig - twenty-five
9. füttern - to feed
10. das Geld - money
11. die Genesung, Rehabilitation - rehabilitation
12. gesäubert - cleaned
13. gesund pflegen - to rehabilitate

14. informieren, mitteilen - to inform
15. der Journalist - journalist
16. die Kontrolle - control
17. die Küste - shore
18. lachen - to laugh
19. lenken - to steer
20. liebe - dear
21. links - left
22. der Mörder - killer
23. morgen - tomorrow
24. nie - never
25. das Öl - oil
26. passieren - to happen, passiert - happened
27. rechts - right
28. die Rede - speech
29. retten - to rescue
30. der Rettungsdienst - rescue service
31. (hinunter)schlucken - to swallow
32. schwimmen - to swim
33. die Situation - situation
34. Spaß haben, genießen - enjoy
35. der Tanker - tanker
36. treiben - floating
37. der Unfall - accident
38. der Vogel - bird
39. vor - ago; vor einem Jahr - a year ago
40. der Wal - whale, der Schwertwal - killer whale
41. waren - were
42. der Wind - wind
43. wollte - wanted
44. wunderbar - wonderful

## B

### Stefan und Mike waschen den Laster (Teil 2)

Der Laster treibt langsam weiter aufs Meer und schaukelt auf den Wellen wie ein kleines Schiff.

Stefan lenkt nach links und nach rechts, während er auf die Bremse und aufs Gas tritt. Aber er kann den Laster nicht kontrollieren. Ein starker Wind trägt ihn die Küste entlang. Stefan und Mike wissen nicht, was sie tun sollen. Sie sitzen einfach da und schauen aus dem Fenster. Das Meerwasser beginnt, in den Laster zu laufen.

„Lass uns nach draußen gehen und uns aufs Dach setzen", sagt Mike.

Sie setzen sich aufs Dach.

### *Stefan and Mike wash the truck (part 2)*

*The truck is floating slowly further in the sea pitching on the waves like a little ship.*

*Stefan is steering to the left and to the right stepping on the brake and gas. But he cannot control the truck. A strong wind is pushing it along the seashore. Stefan and Mike do not know what to do. They are just sitting, looking out of the windows. The sea water begins to run inside.*

*"Let's go out and sit on the roof," Mike says.*

*They sit on the roof.*

*"What will Mr. Schmidt say, I wonder?"*

„Ich frage mich, was Herr Schmidt sagen wird", sagt Mike.

*Mike says.*

Der Laster treibt langsam etwa zwanzig Meter von der Küste entfernt. Einige Leute an der Küste bleiben stehen und schauen verwundert.

*The truck is floating slowly about twenty meters away from the shore. Some people on the shore stop and look at it in surprise.*

„Herr Schmidt wird uns wohl feuern", antwortet Stefan.

*"Mr. Schmidt may fire us," Stefan answers.*

In der Zwischenzeit kommt der Direktor der Universität, Herr Bauer, in sein Büro. Die Sekretärin sagt ihm, dass es heute eine Feier gibt. Sie werden zwei Vögel nach deren Genesung freisetzen. Arbeiter des Rehabilitationszentrums haben sie nach dem Unfall mit dem Tanker Gran Pollución von Öl gesäubert. Der Unfall passierte vor einem Monat. Herr Bauer muss dort eine Rede halten. Die Feier beginnt in fünfundzwanzig Minuten.

*Meanwhile the head of the college Mr. Bauer comes to his office. The secretary says to him that there will be a ceremony today. They will set free two sea birds after rehabilitation. Workers of the rehabilitation centre cleaned oil off them after the accident with the tanker Gran Pollución. The accident happened one month ago. Mr. Bauer must make a speech there. The ceremony begins in twenty-five minutes.*

Herr Bauer und seine Sekretärin nehmen ein Taxi und kommen nach zehn Minuten am Ort der Feier an. Die zwei Vögel sind bereits da. Jetzt sind sie nicht so weiß wie normalerweise. Aber sie können wieder schwimmen und fliegen. Es sind viele Menschen, Journalisten und Fotografen da. Zwei Minuten später beginnt die Feier. Herr Bauer beginnt seine Rede.

*Mr. Bauer and his secretary take a taxi and in ten minutes arrive to the place of the ceremony. These two birds are already there. Now they are not so white as usually. But they can swim and fly again now. There are many people, journalists, photographers there now. In two minutes the ceremony begins. Mr. Bauer begins his speech.*

„Liebe Freunde", sagt er. „Vor einem Monat passierte an dieser Stelle der Unfall mit dem Tanker Gran Pollución. Wir müssen jetzt viele Vögel und Tiere gesund pflegen. Das kostet viel Geld. Die Rehabilitation dieser zwei Vögel zum Beispiel kostet 5000 Euro. Und es freut mich, Ihnen mitteilen zu können, dass diese zwei wunderbaren Vögel nach einem Monat Rehabilitation freigesetzt werden."

*"Dear friends!" he says. "The accident with the tanker Gran Pollución happened at this place a month ago. We must rehabilitate many birds and animals now. It costs a lot of money. For example the rehabilitation of each of these birds costs 5,000 dollars! And I am glad to inform you now that after one month of rehabilitation these two wonderful birds will be set free."*

Zwei Männer nehmen die Kiste mit den Vögeln, bringen sie zum Wasser und öffnen sie. Die Vögel kommen aus der Kiste, springen ins Wasser und schwimmen. Die Fotografen machen Fotos. Die Journalisten befragen Arbeiter des Rehabilitationszentrums über die Tiere.

*Two men take a box with the birds, bring it to the water and open it. The birds go out of the box and then jump in the water and swim. The photographers take pictures. The journalists ask workers of the rehabilitation centre about the animals.*

Plötzlich taucht ein großer Schwertwal auf, schluckt schnell die zwei Vögel hinunter und

*Suddenly a big killer whale comes up, quickly swallows those two birds and goes*

verschwindet wieder. Alle Leute schauen auf die Stelle, an der die Vögel zuvor gewesen waren. Der Direktor der Universität traut seinen Augen nicht. Der Schwertwal taucht wieder auf und sucht nach mehr Vögeln. Da es keine Vögel mehr gibt, verschwindet er wieder. Herr Bauer muss seine Rede beenden.

*down again. All the people look at the place where the birds were before. The head of the college does not believe his eyes. The killer whale comes up again looking for more birds. As there are no other birds there, it goes down again. Mr. Bauer must finish his speech now.*

„Ähm...“, er sucht nach passenden Worten. „Der wundervolle, beständige Fluss des Lebens hört nie auf. Größere Tiere essen kleinere Tiere und so weiter...ähm..was ist das?“, fragt er aufs Wasser schauend. Alle schauen aufs Wasser und sehen einen großen Laster, der die Küste entlang treibt und auf den Wellen schaukelt wie ein Schiff. Zwei Jungen sitzen auf ihm und schauen zum Platz der Feier.

*"Ah...," he chooses suitable words. "The wonderful constant flow of life never stops. Bigger animals eat smaller animals and so on... ah... what is that?" he says looking at the water. All the people look there and see a big truck floating along the shore pitching on the waves like a ship. Two guys sit on it looking at the place of the ceremony.*

„Hallo Herr Bauer“, sagt Mike. „Warum füttern Sie Schwertwale mit Vögeln?“

*"Hello Mr. Bauer," Mike says. "Why are you feeding killer whales with birds?"*

„Hallo Mike“, antwortet Herr Bauer. „Was macht ihr da, Jungs?“

*"Hello Mike," Mr. Bauer answers. "What are you doing there boys?"*

„Wir wollten den Laster waschen“, sagt Stefan.

*"We wanted to wash the truck," Stefan answers.*

„Alles klar“, sagt Herr Bauer. Einige Leute beginnen, an der Situation ihren Spaß zu haben. Sie fangen an, zu lachen.

*"I see," Mr. Bauer says. Some of the people begin to enjoy this situation. They begin to laugh.*

„Gut, ich rufe jetzt den Rettungsdienst. Der wird euch aus dem Wasser holen. Und ich möchte euch morgen in meinem Büro sehen“, sagt der Direktor der Universität und ruft den Rettungsdienst.

*"Well, I will call the rescue service now. They will get you out of the water. And I want to see you in my office tomorrow," the head of the college says and calls the rescue service.*

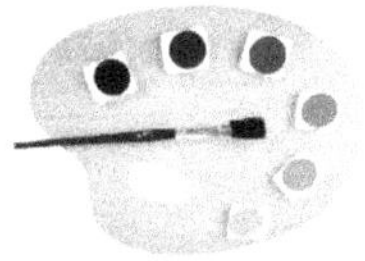

# 21

## Eine Unterrichtsstunde

*A lesson*

## A

**Vokabeln**

1. andere - else
2. die Aufmerksamkeit - attention
   achten auf - pay attention to
3. ausgeben, verwenden - to spend
4. bleiben - to remain
5. der, die, das (Konj.) - which
6. das Ding, die Sache - thing
   diese Dinge - this stuff
7. die Eltern - parent
8. der Fernseher - television
9. der Freund - boyfriend
10. die Freundin - girlfriend
11. die Gesundheit - health
12. das Glück - happiness
13. immer - always
14. die Kinder - children

15. die Klasse - class
16. klein - small
17. der Krug - jar
18. sich kümmern um - to care
19. leer - empty
20. leicht - slightly
21. medizinisch - medical
22. noch, weiterhin - still
23. ohne - without
    wortlos - without a word
24. der Sand - sand
25. schütten - to pour
26. stattdessen - instead
27. der Stein - stone
28. verlieren - to loose
29. weniger - less
30. wichtig - important
31. wirklich - really
32. zwischen - between

## B

### Eine Unterrichtsstunde

Der Direktor der Universität steht vor der Klasse. Auf dem Tisch vor ihm liegen Kisten und andere Dinge. Als der Unterricht beginnt, nimmt er einen großen, leeren Krug und füllt ihn wortlos mit großen Steinen.

„Meint ihr, dass der Krug schon voll ist?“, fragt Herr Bauer die Studenten.

„Ja, das ist er“, stimmen die Studenten zu.

Da nimmt er eine Kiste mit sehr kleinen Steinen und schüttet sie in den Krug. Er schüttelt den Krug leicht. Die kleinen Steine füllen natürlich den Platz zwischen den großen Steinen.

„Was meint ihr jetzt? Der Krug ist voll, oder nicht?“, fragt Herr Bauer sie wieder.

„Ja, das ist er. Er ist jetzt voll“, stimmen die Studenten wieder zu. Der Unterricht beginnt, ihnen Spaß zu machen. Sie lachen.

Da nimmt Herr Bauer eine Kiste mit Sand und schüttet ihn in den Krug. Der Sand füllt natürlich den restlichen Platz.

### *A lesson*

*The head of the college is standing before the class. There are some boxes and other things on the table before him. When the lesson begins he takes a big empty jar and without a word fills it up with big stones.*

*"Do you think the jar is already full?" Mr. Bauer asks students.*

*"Yes, it is," agree students.*

*Then he takes a box with very small stones and pours them into the jar. He shakes the jar slightly. The little stones, of course, fill up the room between the big stones.*

*"What do you think now? The jar is already full, isn't it?" Mr. Bauer asks them again.*

*"Yes, it is. It is full now," the students agree again. They begin to enjoy this lesson. They begin to laugh.*

*Then Mr. Bauer takes a box of sand and pours it into the jar. Of course, the sand fills up all the other room.*

„Jetzt möchte ich, dass ihr in diesem Krug das Leben seht. Die großen Steine sind wichtige Dinge - eure Familie, eure Freundin oder euer Freund, Gesundheit, Kinder, Eltern - Dinge, die euer Leben, wenn ihr alles verliert und nur sie bleiben, weiterhin füllen. Kleine Steine sind andere Dinge, die weniger wichtig sind. Dinge wie euer Haus, Job, Auto. Der Sand ist alles andere - die kleinen Dinge. Wenn ihr zuerst Sand in den Krug füllt, bleibt kein Platz für kleine oder große Steine. Das Gleiche gilt fürs Leben. Wenn ihr eure ganze Zeit und Energie für die kleinen Dinge verwendet, werdet ihr nie Platz für die Dinge haben, die euch wichtig sind. Achtet auf Dinge, die für euer Glück am wichtigsten sind. Spielt mit euren Kindern oder Eltern. Nehmt euch die Zeit für medizinische Untersuchungen. Geht mit eurer Freundin oder eurem Freund ins Café. Es wird immer Zeit bleiben, um zu arbeiten, das Haus zu putzen oder fernzusehen", sagt Herr Bauer. „Kümmert euch erst um die großen Steine - um die Dinge, die wirklich wichtig sind. Alles andere ist nur Sand", er schaut die Studenten an. „Nun, Mike und Stefan, was ist euch wichtiger - einen Laster zu waschen oder euer Leben? Ihr treibt auf einem Laster im Meer wie auf einem Schiff, nur weil ihr den Laster waschen wolltet. Glaubt ihr, dass es keine andere Möglichkeit gibt, ihn zu waschen?"

„Nein, das glauben wir nicht", sagt Stefan.

„Man kann einen Laster stattdessen in einer Waschanlage waschen, nicht wahr?", sagt Herr Bauer.

„Ja, das kann man", sagen die Studenten.

„Ihr müsst immer erst nachdenken, bevor ihr handelt. Ihr müsst euch immer um die großen Steine kümmern, okay?"

„Ja, das müssen wir", antworten die Studenten.

*"Now I want that you to think about this jar like a man's life. The big stones are important things - your family, your girlfriend and boyfriend, your health, your children, your parents - things that if you loose everything and only they remain, your life still will be full. Little stones are other things which are less important. They are things like your house, your job, your car. Sand is everything else - small stuff. If you put sand in the jar at first, there will be no room for little or big stones. The same goes for life. If you spend all of your time and energy on the small stuff, you will never have room for things that are important to you. Pay attention to things that are most important to your happiness. Play with your children or parents. Take time to get medical tests. Take your girlfriend or boyfriend to a café. There will be always time to go to work, clean the house and watch television," Mr. Bauer says. "Take care of the big stones first - things that are really important. Everything else is just sand," he looks at the students. "Now Mike and Stefan, what is more important to you - washing a truck or your lives? You float on a truck in the sea like on a ship just because you wanted to wash the truck. Do you think there is no other way to wash it?"*

*"No, we do not think so," Stefan says.*

*"You can wash a truck in a washing station instead, can't you?" says Mr. Bauer.*

*"Yes, we can," say the students.*

*"You must always think before you do something. You must always take care of the big stones, right?"*

*"Yes, we must," answer the students.*

# 22

## Alexander arbeitet in einem Verlag

*Alexander works at a publishing house*

## A

**Vokabeln**

1. ablehnen - to refuse
2. der Anrufbeantworter - answering machine
3. anrufen - to call
4. aufnehmen - to record
5. bekommen - to get
6. der Beruf - profession
7. da, weil - since, as
8. draußen - outdoors
9. dreißig - thirty
10. dunkel - dark
11. entwerfen, verfassen - to compose
12. entwickeln - to develop
13. der Entwurf, der Text - composition
14. die Fähigkeit - skill
15. fertig - ready
16. die Firma - company

17. die Geschichte - story
18. hallo - hi
19. herstellen - to produce
20. kalt - cold (adj)
    die Kälte - coldness
21. die Koordination - co-ordination
22. kreativ - creative
23. der Kunde - customer
24. laufen - walking
25. lustig - funny
26. der Mensch - human
27. möglich - possible
    so oft wie möglich - as often as possible
28. die Nase - nose
29. nichts - nothing
30. niemand - nobody
31. der Piepton - beep
32. die Regel - rule
33. der Regen - rain
34. schlafen - sleeping
35. schwer - difficult
36. spielen - playing
37. der Text - text
38. traurig - sad
39. die Treppe - stairs
40. sich unterhalten - to talk
41. usw. - etc.
42. verkaufen - to sell
43. verschieden - different
44. vor allem - especially
45. die Welt - world
46. wenigstens - at least
47. die Zeitschrift - magazine
48. die Zeitung - newspaper
49. zukünftig - future

## B

### Alexander arbeitet in einem Verlag

Alexander arbeitet als junger Helfer im Verlag „All-Round“. Er erledigt Schreibarbeiten.

„Alexander, unsere Firma heißt ‚All-Round‘“, sagt der Firmenchef Herr Stark. „Und das heißt, dass wir für jeden Kunden jede Art von Text und Design entwickeln können. Wir bekommen viele Aufträge von Zeitungen, Zeitschriften und anderen Kunden. Alle Aufträge sind verschieden, aber wir lehnen nie einen ab.„

Alexander mag diesen Job sehr, da er kreative Fähigkeiten entwickeln kann. Kreative Arbeit wie Schreiben und Design gefällt ihm. Da er

### *Alexander works at a publishing house*

*Alexander works as a young helper at the publishing house All-round. He does writing work.*

*"Alexander, our firm's name is All-round," the head of the firm Mr. Stark says. "And this means we can do any text composition and design work for any customer. We get many orders from newspapers, magazines and from other customers. All of the orders are different but we never refuse any."*

*Alexander likes this job a lot because he can develop creative skills. He enjoys creative*

Design an der Universität studiert, ist es ein passender Job für seinen zukünftigen Beruf.

*works like writing compositions and design. Since he studies design at college it is a very suitable job for his future profession.*

Heute hat Herr Stark neue Aufgaben für ihn.

*Mr. Stark has some new tasks for him today.*

„Wir haben einige Aufträge. Du kannst zwei davon erledigen“, sagt Herr Stark. „Der erste Auftrag ist von einer Telefonfirma. Sie stellen Telefone mit Anrufbeantwortern her. Sie brauchen ein paar lustige Texte für die Anrufbeantworter. Nichts verkauft sich besser als etwas Lustiges. Entwirf bitte vier, fünf Texte.“

*"We have some orders. You can do two of them," Mr. Stark says. "The first order is from a telephone company. They produce telephones with answering machines. They need some funny texts for answering machines. Nothing sells better than funny things. Compose four or five texts, please."*

„Wie lang sollen sie sein?“, fragt Alexander.

*"How long must they be?" Alexander asks.*

„Sie können fünf bis dreißig Wörter haben“, antwortet Herr Stark. „Der zweite Auftrag ist von der Zeitung ‚Grüne Welt‘. Diese Zeitung schreibt über Tiere, Vögel, Fische usw. Sie brauchen einen Text über irgendein Haustier. Er kann lustig oder traurig sein oder einfach eine Geschichte über dein eigenes Haustier. Hast du ein Haustier?“

*"They can be from five to thirty words," Mr. Stark answers. "And the second order is from the magazine 'Green world'. This magazine writes about animals, birds, fish etc. They need a text about any home animal. It can be funny or sad, or just a story about your own animal. Do you have an animal?"*

„Ja, ich habe eine Katze. Sie heißt Minka“, antwortet Alexander. „Und ich denke, ich kann eine Geschichte über ihre Streiche schreiben. Wann sollen die Texte fertig sein?“

*"Yes, I do. I have a cat. Its name is Minka," Alexander answers. "And I think I can write a story about its tricks. When must it be ready?"*

„Diese zwei Aufträge sollen bis morgen fertig sein“, antwortet Herr Stark.

*"These two orders must be ready by tomorrow," Mr. Stark answers.*

„Gut. Kann ich anfangen?“, fragt Alexander.

*"Okay. May I begin now?" Alexander asks.*

„Ja“, sagt Herr Stark.

*"Yes, Alexander," Mr. Stark says.*

Alexander bringt die Texte am nächsten Tag. Er hat fünf Texte für den Anrufbeantworter. Herr Stark liest sie:

*Alexander brings those texts the next day. He has five texts for the answering machines. Mr. Stark reads them:*

1. „Hallo. Jetzt musst du etwas sagen.“

*1. "Hi. Now you say something."*

2. „Hallo, ich bin ein Anrufbeantworter. Und was bist du?“

*2. "Hello. I am an answering machine. And what are you?"*

3. „Hallo. Außer meinem Anrufbeantworter ist gerade niemand zuhause. Du kannst dich mit ihm unterhalten. Warte auf den Piepton.“

*3. "Hi. Nobody is at home now but my answering machine is. So you can talk to it instead of me. Wait for the beep."*

4. „Das ist kein Anrufbeantworter. Das ist ein Gedankenaufnahmegerät. Nach dem Piepton

*4. "This is not an answering machine. This is a thought-recording machine. After the beep,*

denke an deinen Namen, den Grund, aus dem du anrufst, und die Nummer, unter der ich dich zurückrufen kann. Und ich werde darüber nachdenken, ob ich dich zurückrufe."

*think about your name, your reason for calling and a number which I can call you back. And I will think about calling you back."*

5. „Sprechen Sie nach dem Piepton! Sie haben das Recht, Ihre Aussage zu verweigern. Ich werde alles, was Sie sagen, aufzeichnen und verwenden."

*5. "Speak after the beep! You have the right to be silent. I will record and use everything you say."*

„Nicht schlecht. Und was ist mit den Tieren?", fragt Herr Stark. Alexander gibt ihm ein anderes Blatt. Herr Stark liest:

*"It is not bad. And what about animals?" Mr. Stark asks. Alexander gives him another sheet of paper. Mr. Stark reads:*

**Regeln für Katzen**

***Some rules for cats***

Laufen:

*Walking:*

Renne so oft wie möglich schnell und nahe an einem Menschen vorbei, vor allem: auf Treppen, wenn sie etwas tragen, im Dunkeln und wenn sie morgens aufstehen. Das trainiert ihre Koordination.

*As often as possible, run quickly and as close as possible in front of a human, especially: on stairs, when they have something on their hands, in the dark, and when they get up in the morning. This will train their co-ordination.*

Im Bett:

*In bed:*

Schlafe nachts immer auf dem Menschen, damit er sich nicht umdrehen kann. Versuche, auf seinem Gesicht zu liegen. Vergewissere dich, dass dein Schwanz genau auf seiner Nase liegt.

*Always sleep on a human at night. So he or she cannot turn in the bed. Try to lie on his or her face. Make sure that your tail is right on their nose.*

Schlafen:

*Sleeping:*

Um genug Energie zum Spielen zu haben, muss eine Katze viel schlafen (mindestens 16 Stunden am Tag). Es ist nicht schwer, einen passenden Schlafplatz zu finden. Jeder Platz, an dem ein Mensch gerne sitzt, ist gut. Draußen gibt es auch viele gute Plätze. Du kannst sie aber nicht verwenden, wenn es regnet oder kalt ist. Du kannst stattdessen das offene Fenster verwenden.

*To have a lot of energy for playing, a cat must sleep a lot (at least 16 hours per day). It is not difficult to find a suitable place to sleep. Any place where a human likes to sit is good. There are good places outdoors too. But you cannot use them when it rains or when it is cold. You can use open windows instead.*

Herr Stark lacht.

*Mr. Stark laughs.*

„Gute Arbeit, Alexander! Ich denke, die Zeitung ‚Grüne Welt' wird deinen Entwurf mögen", sagt er.

*"Good work, Alexander! I think the magazine 'Green world' will like your composition," he says.*

# 23

## Katzenregeln

*Cat rules*

## A

### Vokabeln

1. das Bein - leg
2. beißen - to bite
3. bekommen - to get
4. die Chance - chance
5. denken - thinking
6. ein paar - few
7. etwas, nichts - anything
8. der Gast - guest
9. das Geheimnis - secret
10. die Hausaufgaben - homework
11. hinter - behind
12. die (Jahres)zeit - season
13. das Kind - child
14. kochend - cooking
15. küssen - to kiss
16. lecker - tasty

17. lesend - reading
18. die Liebe - love,
    lieben - to love
19. manchmal, ab und zu - sometimes
20. obwohl, trotzdem - although
21. die Panik - panic
    in Panik versetzen - to panic
22. der Planet - planet
23. das Rätsel - mystery
24. reiben - to rub
25. der Schritt - step,
    treten - to step
26. die Schule - school
27. der Spaß - fun
28. die Stechmücke - mosquito
29. stehlen - to steal
30. die Tastatur - keyboard
31. der Teller - plate
32. die Toilette - toilet
33. vergessen - to forget
34. sich verstecken - to hide
    das Versteckspiel - hide-and-seek
35. vorgeben; so tun, als ob - to pretend
36. weglaufen - run away
37. das Wetter - weather

## B

### Katzenregeln

„Die Zeitschrift ‚Grüne Welt' hat uns einen neuen Auftrag erteilt", sagt Herr Stark am nächsten Tag zu Alexander. „Und dieser Auftrag ist für dich. Ihnen hat dein Entwurf gefallen und sie wollen einen längeren Text über ‚Katzenregeln'."

Alexander braucht zwei Tage für diesen Text. Hier ist er.

### Geheime Regeln für Katzen

Obwohl Katzen die besten und wundervollsten Tiere auf diesem Planeten sind, tun sie manchmal sehr seltsame Dinge. Einem Menschen ist es gelungen, ein paar Katzengeheimnisse zu stehlen. Es sind Lebensregeln, um die Weltherrschaft zu übernehmen! Es bleibt jedoch ein Rätsel, wie diese Regeln den Katzen helfen sollen.

Badezimmer:

Gehe immer mit Gästen ins Badezimmer und auf die Toilette. Du musst nichts tun. Sitze einfach

### *Cat rules*

*"The magazine 'Green world' places a new order," Mr. Stark says to Alexander next day. "And this order is for you, Alexander. They like your composition and they want a bigger text about 'Cat rules'."*

*It takes Alexander two days to compose this text. Here it is.*

### *Some secret rules for cats*

*Although cats are the best and the most wonderful animals on this planet, they sometimes do very strange things. One of the humans managed to steal some cat secrets. They are some rules of life in order to take over the world! But how these rules will help cats is still a total mystery to the humans.*

*Bathrooms:*

*Always go with guests to the bathroom and*

nur da, schaue sie an und reibe dich ab und zu an ihren Beinen.

Türen:

Alle Türen müssen offen sein. Um eine Tür zu öffnen, stelle dich mit einem traurigen Blick vor den Menschen. Wenn er eine Tür öffnet, musst du nicht durchgehen. Wenn du auf diese Weise die Haustür geöffnet hast, bleibe in der Tür stehen und denke nach. Das ist vor allem wichtig, wenn es sehr kalt ist oder regnet oder in der Stechmückenzeit.

Kochen:

Setze dich immer genau hinter den rechten Fuß von kochenden Menschen. So können sie dich nicht sehen und die Chance ist größer, dass sie auf dich treten. Wenn das passiert, nehmen sie dich auf den Arm und geben dir etwas Leckeres zu essen.

Lesen:

Versuche, nahe an das Gesicht der lesenden Person zu kommen, zwischen Augen und Buch. Am besten ist es, sich auf das Buch zu legen.

Hausaufgaben der Kinder:

Lege dich auf Bücher und Hefte und tue so, als ob du schläfst. Springe von Zeit zu Zeit auf den Stift. Beiße, falls ein Kind versucht, dich vom Tisch zu verscheuchen.

Computer:

Wenn ein Mensch am Computer arbeitet, springe auf den Tisch und laufe über die Tastatur.

Essen:

Katzen müssen viel essen. Aber Essen ist nur der halbe Spaß. Die andere Hälfte ist, das Essen zu bekommen. Wenn Menschen essen, lege deinen Schwanz auf ihren Teller, wenn sie nicht hinschauen. Damit vergrößerst du deine Chancen, einen ganzen Teller Essen zu bekommen. Iss nie von deinem eigenen Teller, wenn du Essen vom Tisch nehmen kannst. Trink nie aus deiner

*to the toilet. You do not need to do anything. Just sit, look and sometimes rub their legs.*

*Doors:*

*All doors must be open. To get a door opened, stand looking sad at humans. When they open a door, you need not go through it. After you open in this way the outside door, stand in the door and think about something. This is especially important when the weather is very cold, or when it is a rainy day, or when it is the mosquito season.*

*Cooking:*

*Always sit just behind the right foot of cooking humans. So they cannot see you and you have a better chance that a human steps on you. When it happens, they take you in their hands and give something tasty to eat.*

*Reading books:*

*Try to get closer to the face of a reading human, between eyes and the book. The best is to lie on the book.*

*Children's school homework:*

*Lie on books and copy-books and pretend to sleep. But from time to time jump on the pen. Bite if a child tries to take you away from the table.*

*Computer:*

*If a human works with a computer, jump up on the desk and walk over the keyboard.*

*Food:*

*Cats need to eat a lot. But eating is only half of the fun. The other half is getting the food. When humans eat, put your tail in their plate when they do not look. It will give you a better chance to get a full plate of food. Never eat from your own plate if*

eigenen Schüssel, wenn du aus der Tasse eines Menschen trinken kannst.

*you can take some food from the table. Never drink from your own water plate if you can drink from a human's cup.*

Verstecken:

*Hiding:*

Verstecke dich an Orten, an denen dich Menschen ein paar Tage lang nicht finden können. Das wird die Menschen in Panik versetzen (was sie lieben), weil sie glauben, dass du weggelaufen bist. Wenn du aus deinem Versteck hervorkommst, werden sie dich küssen und dir ihre Liebe zeigen. Und du bekommst vielleicht etwas Leckeres.

*Hide in places where humans cannot find you for a few days. This will make humans panic (which they love) thinking that you ran away. When you come out of the hiding place, the humans will kiss you and show their love. And*

*you may get something tasty.*

Menschen:

*Humans:*

Die Aufgabe des Menschen ist, uns zu füttern, mit uns zu spielen und unsere Kiste sauber zu machen. Es ist wichtig, dass sie nicht vergessen, wer der Chef im Haus ist.

*Tasks of humans are to feed us, to play with us, and to clean our box. It is important that they do not forget who the head of the house is.*

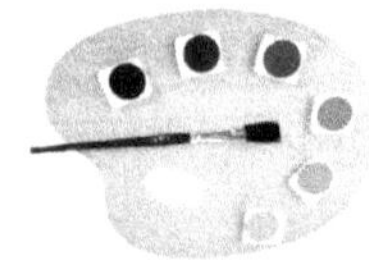

# 24

# Gruppenarbeit

*Teamwork*

## A

**Vokabeln**

1. arbeitend - working
2. der Außerirdische - alien
3. bald - soon
4. beendete - stopped
5. begann - began
6. beibringen - to teach
7. bewegte sich - moved
8. Billionen - billion
9. bis - until
10. die Blume - flower
11. einer von euch - either of you
12. die Erde - earth
13. erinnerte sich - remembered
14. fallen - to fall,
    fiel - fell
15. der Fernseher - TV-set
16. fertig - finished
17. flog weg - flew away
18. fortführen - to continue;
    weiter schauen - continued to watch
19. der Garten - garden

20. gegen - against
21. geliebt - loved
22. hatte - had
23. Haupt-, zentral - central
24. hörte - heard
25. informierte - informed
26. er kam, gekommen - came
27. der Kapitän - captain
28. der Kollege - colleague
29. der Krieg - war
30. kurz - short
31. lächelte - smiled
32. der Laser - laser
33. machte an - switched on
34. der Radar - radar
35. das Radio - radio
36. das Raumschiff - spaceship
37. richtete - pointed
38. sagte - said
39. schaute - looked
40. die Serie - serial
41. sterben - to die,
    starb - died
42. tanzen - to dance;
    getanzt (Part.) - danced
    tanzend - dancing
43. tausend - thousand
44. teilnehmen - to take part
45. tötete, getötet (Part.) - killed
46. verlassen (Part.) - went away
47. wackelte - shook
48. das Weltall - space
49. wunderschön - beautiful
50. wusste - knew
51. zerstören - destroy

## B

### Gruppenarbeit

Stefan will Journalist werden. Er studiert an der Universität. Heute hat er einen Schreibkurs. Herr Bauer bringt den Studenten bei, Artikel zu schreiben.

„Liebe Freunde“, sagt er, „ein paar von euch werden für Verlage, Zeitungen oder Zeitschriften, das Radio oder das Fernsehen arbeiten. Das bedeutet, dass ihr in einer Gruppe arbeiten werdet. Es ist nicht einfach, in einer Gruppe zu arbeiten. Ich möchte, dass ihr jetzt versucht, in einer Gruppe einen journalistischen Text zu schreiben. Ich brauche einen Jungen und ein

### *Team work*

*Stefan wants to be a journalist. He studies at a college. He has a composition lesson today. Mr. Bauer teaches students to write composition.*

*"Dear friends," he says, "some of you will work for publishing houses, newspapers or magazines, the radio or television. This means you will work in a team. Working in a team is not simple. Now I want that you try to make a journalistic composition in a team. I need a boy and a girl."*

Mädchen."

Viele Studenten wollen bei der Gruppenarbeit mitmachen. Herr Bauer wählt Stefan und Carol. Carol kommt aus den USA, aber sie spricht sehr gut Deutsch.

„Setzt auch bitte an diesen Tisch. Ihr seid jetzt Kollegen", sagt Herr Bauer zu ihnen. „Ihr werdet einen kurzen Text schreiben. Einer von euch beginnt den Text und gibt ihn dann seinem Kollegen. Der Kollege liest den Text und führt ihn dann fort. Dann gibt euer Kollege ihn zurück, der Erste liest ihn und führt ihn fort. Und so weiter, bis die Zeit vorbei ist. Ihr habt zwanzig Minuten."

Herr Bauer gibt ihnen Papier und Carol fängt an. Sie denkt kurz nach und schreibt dann.

**Gruppenarbeit**

Carol: Julia sah aus dem Fenster. Die Blumen in ihrem Garten bewegten sich im Wind, als ob sie tanzten. Sie erinnerte sich an den Abend, an dem sie mit Billy getanzt hatte. Das war vor einem Jahr, aber sie erinnerte sich an alles - seine blauen Augen, sein Lächeln, seine Stimme. Das war eine glückliche Zeit für sie gewesen, aber die war nun vorbei. Warum war er nicht bei ihr?

Stefan: Zu dieser Zeit war Raumschiffkapitän Billy Brisk in seinem Raumschiff White Star. Er hatte eine wichtige Mission und keine Zeit, über dieses dumme Mädchen, mit dem er vor einem Jahr getanzt hatte, nachzudenken. Schnell richtete er den Laser der White Star auf Raumschiffe Außerirdischer. Dann stellte er das Funkgerät an und sprach zu den Außerirdischen: „Ihr habt eine Stunde, um aufzugeben. Wenn ihr in einer Stunde nicht aufgebt, werde ich euch zerstören." Kurz bevor er seine Rede beendet hatte, traf jedoch ein Laser der Außerirdischen den linken Motor der White Star. Billys Laser begann, auf die Raumschiffe der Außerirdischen zu schießen, und gleichzeitig schaltete Billy den Hauptmotor und den rechten Motor an. Der Laser der Außerirdischen zerstörte den funktionierenden rechten Motor und die White Star wackelte stark.

*Many students want to take part in the team work. Mr. Bauer chooses Stefan and Carol. Carol is from the USA but she can speak German very well.*

*"Please, sit at this table. Now you are colleagues," Mr. Bauer says to them. "You will write a short composition. Either of you will begin the composition and then give it to your colleague. Your colleague will read the composition and continue it. Then your colleague will give it back and the first one will read and continue it. And so on until your time is over. I give you twenty minutes."*

*Mr. Bauer gives them paper and Carol begins. She thinks a little and then writes.*

***Team composition***

*Carol: Julia was looking through the window. The flowers in her garden were moving in the wind as if dancing. She remembered that evening when she danced with Billy. It was a year ago but she remembered everything - his blue eyes, his smile and his voice. It was a happy time for her but it was over now. Why was not he with her?*

*Stefan: At this moment space captain Billy Brisk was at the spaceship White Star. He had an important task and he did not have time to think about that silly girl who he danced with a year ago. He quickly pointed the lasers of White Star at alien spaceships. Then he switched on the radio and talked to the aliens: "I give you an hour to give up. If in one hour you do not give up I will destroy you." But before he finished an alien laser hit the left engine of the White Star. Billy's laser began to hit alien spaceships and at the same time he switched on the central and the right engines. The alien laser destroyed the working right engine and the White Star*

Billy fiel auf den Boden und überlegte währenddessen, welches der Raumschiffe der Außerirdischen er zuerst zerstören müsse.

*shook badly. Billy fell on the floor thinking during the fall which of the alien spaceships he must destroy first.*

Carol: Aber er schlug mit seinem Kopf auf dem metallenen Boden auf und war sofort tot. Bevor er starb, dachte er noch an das arme schöne Mädchen, das ihn liebte, und es tat ihm sehr leid, dass er sie verlassen hatte. Kurz darauf beendeten die Menschen den dummen Krieg gegen die armen Außerirdischen. Sie zerstörten alle ihre eigenen Raumschiffe und Laser und informierten die Außerirdischen, dass die Menschen nie wieder einen Krieg gegen sie beginnen würden. Die Menschen sagten, sie wollten Freunde der Außerirdischen sein. Julia war sehr froh, als sie davon hörte. Dann machte sie den Fernseher an und schaute eine tolle deutsche Serie weiter.

*Carol: But he hit his head on the metal floor and died at the same moment. But before he died he remembered the poor beautiful girl who loved him and he was very sorry that he went away from her. Soon people stopped this silly war on poor aliens. They destroyed all of their own spaceships and lasers and informed the aliens that people would never start a war against them again. People said that they wanted to be friends with the aliens. Julia was very glad when she heard about it. Then she switched on the TV-set and continued to watch a wonderful German serial.*

Stefan: Da die Menschen ihre eigenen Radare und Laser zerstört hatten, wusste niemand, dass Raumschiffe der Außerirdischen der Erde sehr nahe kamen. Tausende Laser der Außerirdischen trafen die Erde und töten die arme, dumme Julia und fünf Billionen Menschen in einer Sekunde. Die Erde war zerstört und ihre Teile flogen in den Weltraum hinaus.

*Stefan: Because people destroyed their own radars and lasers, nobody knew that spaceships of aliens came very close to the Earth. Thousands of aliens' lasers hit the Earth and killed poor silly Julia and five billion people in a second. The Earth was destroyed and its turning parts flew away in space.*

„Wie ich sehe, habt ihr euren Text fertig, bevor die Zeit um ist“, sagte Herr Bauer lächelnd. „Gut, der Unterricht ist vorbei. Lasst uns das nächste Mal diese Gruppenarbeit lesen und darüber sprechen.“

*"I see you came to the finish before your time is over," Mr. Bauer smiled. "Well, the lesson is over. Let us read and speak about this team composition during the next lesson."*

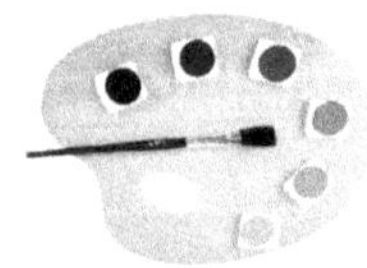

# 25

## Mike und Stefan suchen einen neuen Job

*Mike and Stefan are looking for a new job*

## A

**Vokabeln**

1. die Anzeige - advert
2. das Alter - age
3. der Arzt - doctor
4. der Bauer - farmer
5. bedienen - to serve
6. die Begabung - gift
7. die Beratung - consultancy
8. beurteilen - to estimate
9. dreckig - dirty
10. empfehlen - to recommend;
    die Empfehlung - recommendation
11. das Essen - food

12. der Fragebogen - questionnaire
13. der Führer - leader
14. gefunden - found
15. das Haustier - pet
16. die Idee - idea
17. der Ingenieur - engineer
18. das Inserat - ad
19. das Kätzchen - kitten
20. die Kunst - art
21. der Künstler - artist
22. laut - aloud
23. die Methode - method
24. monoton - monotonous
25. der Nachbar - neighbour
26. die Natur - nature
27. persönlich - personal
28. der Programmierer - programmer
29. die Ratte - rat
30. reisen - to travel
31. die Rubrik - rubric
32. schlau - sly
33. der Schriftsteller - writer
34. der Spaniel - spaniel
35. spanisch - Spanish
36. der Übersetzer - translator
37. der Tierarzt - vet
38. der Traum - dream,
    träumen - to dream
39. während - while
40. der Welpe - puppy

## B

**Mike und Stefan suchen einen neuen Job**

Mike und Stefan sind bei Stefan zuhause. Stefan macht den Tisch nach dem Frühstück sauber und Mike liest Anzeigen und Inserate in der Zeitung. Er liest die Rubrik „Tiere". Stefans Schwester Anke ist auch im Zimmer. Sie versucht, die Katze, die sich unterm Bett versteckt, zu fangen.

„Es gibt so viele kostenlose Tiere in der Zeitung. Ich denke, ich werde mir eine Katze oder einen Hund aussuchen. Was meinst du, Stefan?", fragt Mike Stefan.

„Anke, hör auf, die Katze zu ärgern", sagt Stefan wütend. „Na ja, Mike, das ist keine schlechte Idee. Dein Haustier wartet immer zuhause auf

***Mike and Stefan are looking for a new job***

*Mike and Stefan are at Stefan's home. Stefan is cleaning the table after breakfast and Mike is reading adverts and ads in a newspaper. He is reading the rubric "Animals". Stefan's sister Anke is in the room too. She is trying to catch the cat hiding under the bed.*

*"There are so many pets for free in the newspaper. I think I will choose a cat or a dog. Stefan, what do you think?" Mike asks Stefan.*

*"Anke, do not bother the cat!" Stefan says angrily. "Well Mike, it is not a bad idea. Your pet will always wait for you at home and will*

dich und ist so glücklich, wenn du nach Hause kommst und ihm Futter gibst. Und vergiss nicht, dass du morgens und abends mit deinem Tier Gassi gehen oder seine Kiste sauber machen musst. Manchmal musst du den Boden putzen oder mit dem Tier zum Tierarzt gehen. Also, denk gut darüber nach, bevor du dir ein Haustier anschaffst."

*be so happy when you come back home and give some food. And do not forget that you will have to walk with your pet in mornings and evenings or clean its box. Sometimes you will have to clean the floor or take your pet to a vet. So think carefully before you get an animal."*

„Also, hier sind ein paar Anzeigen. Hör zu", sagt Mike und beginnt, laut vorzulesen:

*"Well, there are some ads here. Listen," Mike says and begins to read aloud:*

„Habe einen dreckigen, weißen Hund gefunden, schaut aus wie eine Ratte. Hat vielleicht lange auf der Straße gelebt. Ich gebe ihn für Geld her."

*"Found dirty white dog, looks like a rat. It may live outside for a long time. I will give it away for money."*

Und hier noch eine:

*Here is one more:*

„Spanischer Hund, spricht Spanisch. Gebe ihn kostenlos ab. Und kostenlose Welpen, halb Spaniel, halb schlauer Nachbarshund."

*"Spanish dog, speaks Spanish. Give away for free. And free puppies half spaniel half sly neighbor's dog."*

Mike schaut Stefan an: „Wie kann ein Hund Spanisch sprechen?"

*Mike looks at Stefan: "How can a dog speak Spanish?"*

„Ein Hund kann Spanisch verstehen. Verstehst du Spanisch?", fragt Stefan grinsend.

*"A dog may understand Spanish. Can you understand Spanish?" Stefan asks smiling.*

„Ich verstehe kein Spanisch. Hör zu, hier ist noch eine Anzeige:

*"I cannot understand Spanish. Listen, here is one more ad:*

Gebe kostenlos Kätzchen vom Bauernhof her. Fertig zum Essen. Sie essen alles."

*"Give away free farm kittens. Ready to eat. They will eat anything."*

Mike blättert die Zeitung um. „Na gut, ich denke, Tiere können warten. Ich suche besser einen Job." Er findet die Stellenanzeigen und liest laut:

*Mike turns the newspaper. "Well, I think pets can wait. I will better look for a job," he finds the rubric about jobs and reads aloud,*

„Suchen Sie nach einem passenden Job? Die Arbeitsvermittlung ‚Passende Mitarbeiter' kann Ihnen helfen. Unsere Berater beurteilen ihre persönliche Begabung und erstellen Ihnen eine Empfehlung für den passendsten Beruf."

*"Are you looking for a suitable job? The job consultancy 'Suitable personnel' can help you. Our consultants will estimate your personal gifts and will give you a recommendation about the most suitable profession."*

Mika schaut auf und sagt: „Was meinst du, Stefan?"

*Mike looks up and says: "Stefan what do you think?"*

„Der beste Job für euch ist, einen Laster im Meer zu waschen und ihn wegschwimmen zu lassen", sagt Anke und rennt dann schnell aus dem Zimmer.

*"The best job for you is washing a truck in the sea and let it float," Anke says and quickly runs out of the room.*

*"It is not a bad idea. Let's go now," Stefan*

„Keine schlechte Idee. Lass uns gleich gehen“, antwortet Stefan und holt vorsichtig die Katze aus dem Kessel, in den Anke sie kurz zuvor gelegt hatte.

*answers and takes carefully the cat out of the kettle, where Anke put the animal a minute ago.*

Mike und Stefan fahren mit dem Fahrrad zur Arbeitsvermittlung „Passende Mitarbeiter“. Es gibt keine Schlange und sie gehen hinein. Zwei Frauen sind da. Eine von ihnen telefoniert. Die andere schreibt etwas. Sie bittet Mike und Stefan, Platz zu nehmen. Sie heißt Frau Habel. Sie fragt sie nach ihren Namen und ihrem Alter.

*Mike and Stefan arrive to the job consultancy "Suitable personnel" by their bikes. There is no queue, so they go inside. There are two women there. One of them is speaking on the telephone. Another woman is writing something. She asks Mike and Stefan to take seats. Her name is Mrs. Habel. She asks them their names and their age.*

„Gut, lasst mich euch die Methode, nach der wir arbeiten, erklären. Schaut, es gibt fünf Berufskategorien:

*"Well, let me explain the method which we use. Look, there are five kinds of professions.*

1. Die Erste ist Mensch - Natur. Berufe: Bauer, Tierpfleger usw.

*1. The first kind is man - nature. Professions: farmer, zoo worker etc.*

2. Die Zweite ist Mensch - Maschine. Berufe: Pilot, Taxifahrer, Lastwagenfahrer usw.

*2. The second kind is man - machine. Professions: pilot, taxi driver, truck driver etc.*

3. Die Dritte ist Mensch - Mensch. Berufe: Arzt, Lehrer, Journalist usw.

*3. The third kind is man - man. Professions: doctor, teacher, journalist etc.*

4. Die Vierte ist Mensch - Computer. Berufe: Übersetzer, Ingenieur, Programmierer usw.

*4. The fourth kind is man - computer. Professions: translator, engineer, programmer etc.*

5. Die Fünfte ist Mensch - Kunst. Berufe: Schriftsteller, Künstler, Sänger usw.

*5. The fifth kind is man - art. Professions: writer, artist, singer etc.*

Wir erstellen Empfehlungen für passende Berufe erst, wenn wir euch besser kennengelernt haben. Lasst mich zuerst eure persönlichen Begabungen beurteilen. Ich muss wissen, was ihr mögt und was ihr nicht mögt. Dann wissen wir, welcher Beruf am besten zu euch passt. Füllt jetzt bitte den Fragebogen aus“, sagt Frau Habel und gibt ihnen die Fragebögen. Stefan und Mike füllen die Fragebögen aus.

*We give recommendations about a suitable profession only when we learn about you more. First let me estimate your personal gifts. I must know what you like and what you dislike. Then we will know which kind of profession is the most suitable for you. Please, fill up the questionnaire now," Mrs. Habel says and gives them the questionnaires. Stefan and Mike fill up the questionnaires.*

Fragebogen
Name: Stefan Müller

Questionnaire
Name: *Stefan Müller*

| | | Mag ich<br>I like | Habe ich nichts dagegen<br>I do not mind | Hasse ich<br>I hate |
|---|---|---|---|---|
| 1. | Maschinen beobachten<br>Watch machines | | √ | |
| 2. | Mit Menschen sprechen<br>Speak with people | √ | | |
| 3. | Kunden bedienen<br>Serve customers | | √ | |
| 4. | Autos, Lastwagen fahren<br>Drive cars, trucks | √ | | |
| 5. | Im Büro arbeiten<br>Work inside | √ | | |
| 6. | Draußen arbeiten<br>Work outside | √ | | |
| 7. | Mir viel merken<br>Remember a lot | | √ | |
| 8. | Reisen<br>Travel | √ | | |
| 9. | Bewerten, kontrollieren<br>Estimate, check | | | √ |
| 10. | Dreckige Arbeit<br>Dirty work | | √ | |
| 11. | Monotone Arbeit<br>Monotonous work | | | √ |
| 12. | Schwere Arbeit<br>Hard work | | √ | |
| 13. | Führer sein<br>Be leader | | √ | |
| 14. | In der Gruppe arbeiten<br>Work in team | | √ | |
| 15. | Während der Arbeit träumen<br>Dream while working | √ | | |
| 16. | Trainieren<br>Train | | √ | |
| 17. | Kreative Arbeit<br>Do creative work | √ | | |
| 18. | Mit Texten arbeiten<br>Work with texts | √ | | |

Fragebogen
Name: Mike Sullivan

Questionnaire
Name: *Mike Sullivan*

| | | Mag ich<br>I like | Habe ich nichts dagegen<br>I do not mind | Hasse ich<br>I hate |
|---|---|---|---|---|
| 1. | Maschinen beobachten<br>Watch machines | | √ | |
| 2. | Mit Menschen sprechen<br>Speak with people | √ | | |
| 3. | Kunden bedienen<br>Serve customers | | √ | |
| 4. | Autos, Lastwagen fahren<br>Drive cars, trucks | | √ | |
| 5. | Im Büro arbeiten<br>Work inside | √ | | |
| 6. | Draußen arbeiten<br>Work outside | √ | | |
| 7. | Mir viel merken<br>Remember a lot | | √ | |
| 8. | Reisen<br>Travel | √ | | |
| 9. | Bewerten, kontrollieren<br>Estimate, check | | √ | |
| 10. | Dreckige Arbeit<br>Dirty work | | √ | |
| 11. | Monotone Arbeit<br>Monotonous work | | | √ |
| 12. | Schwere Arbeit<br>Hard work | | √ | |
| 13. | Führer sein<br>Be leader | | | √ |
| 14. | In der Gruppe arbeiten<br>Work in team | √ | | |
| 15. | Während der Arbeit träumen<br>Dream while working | √ | | |
| 16. | Trainieren<br>Train | | √ | |
| 17. | Kreative Arbeit<br>Do creative work | √ | | |
| 18. | Mit Texten arbeiten<br>Work with texts | √ | | |

# 26

## Bewerbung bei den „Bremerhavener Nachrichten"

*Applying to "Bremerhavener Nachrichten"*

## A

### Vokabeln

1. angekommen - arrived
2. Auf Wiedersehen - goodbye
3. die Ausbildung - education
4. ausgewertet - estimated
5. begleiten - to accompany
6. berichten - to report
   der Reporter - reporter
7. sich bewerben - to apply
8. einundzwanzig - twenty-one
9. empfohlen - recommended
10. das Feld - field
11. die Finanzwissenschaft - finance
12. fließend - fluently
13. das Formular - form
14. Fräulein - Miss
15. gab - gave
16. gearbeitet - worked
17. gefragt - asked
18. das Geschlecht - sex
19. der Herausgeber - editor

20. die Information, die Angabe - information
21. kennengelernt - learned about
22. könnte, kann - could
23. ledig - single
24. leer - blank, empty
25. männlich - male
26. nahm - took
27. die Nationalität - nationality
28. die Patroiulle, die Streife - patrol
29. die Polizei - police
30. siebzehn - seventeen (hour)
31. der Stand - status,
    der Familienstand - family status
32. das Sternchen - asterisk
33. unterstreichen - to underline
34. der Verbrecher - criminal
35. verlassen - to leave
36. weiblich - female
37. die Woche - week
38. der zweite Name - middle name

## B

**Bewerbung bei den „Bremerhavener Nachrichten"**

Frau Habel wertete Stefans und Mikes Antworten im Fragebogen aus. Indem sie ihre persönlichen Begabungen kennenlernte, konnte sie ihnen Empfehlungen für passende Berufe geben. Sie sagte, dass die dritte Berufskategorie am besten zu ihnen passte. Sie könnten als Arzt, Lehrer oder Journalist arbeiten. Frau Habel empfahl ihnen, sich um einen Job bei der Zeitung „Bremerhavener Nachrichten" zu bewerben. Die hatte einen Nebenjob für Studenten zu vergeben, die Polizeiberichte in der Rubrik über Verbrechen verfassen konnten. Also gingen Mike und Stefan in die Personalabteilung der Zeitung „Bremerhavener Nachrichten" und bewarben sich um den Job.

„Wir waren heute bei der Arbeitsvermittlung ‚Passende Mitarbeiter'", sagte Stefan zu Frau Krämer, der Leiterin der Personalabteilung. „Sie haben uns empfohlen, uns bei Ihrer Zeitung zu bewerben."

***Applying to "Bremerhavener Nachrichten"***

*Mrs. Habel estimated Stefan's and Mike's answers in the questionnaires. When she learned about their personal gifts she could give them some recommendations about suitable professions. She said that the third profession kind is the most suitable for them. They could work as a doctor, a teacher or a journalist etc. Mrs. Habel recommended them to apply for a job with the newspaper "Bremerhavener Nachrichten". They gave a part time job to students who could compose police reports for the criminal rubric. So Mike and Stefan arrived at the personnel department of the newspaper "Bremerhavener Nachrichten" and applied for this job.*

*"We have been to the job consultancy 'Suitable personnel' today," Stefan said to Miss Krämer, who was the head of the personnel department. "They have recommended us to apply to your newspaper."*

„Habt ihr schon als Reporter gearbeitet“, fragte Frau Krämer.

*"Well, have you worked as a reporter before?" Miss Krämer asked.*

„Nein, das haben wir noch nicht“, antwortete Stefan.

*"No, we have not," Stefan answered.*

„Füllt bitte diese Formulare mit euren persönlichen Angaben aus“, sagte Frau Krämer und gab ihnen zwei Formulare. Mike und Stefan füllten sie aus.

*"Please, fill up these personal information forms," Miss Krämer said and gave them two forms. Mike and Stefan filled up the personal information forms.*

| **Persönliche Angaben**<br>*Alle mit einem Sternchen * markierten Felder müssen ausgefüllt werden. Die anderen Felder können leer gelassen werden.* | **Personal information form**<br>*You must fill up fields with asterisk *. You can leave other fields blank.* |
|---|---|
| Vorname*<br>First name | Stefan<br>*Stefan* |
| Zweiter Name<br>Middle name | |
| Nachname*<br>Last name | Müller<br>*Müller* |
| Geschlecht*<br>Sex | (unterstreiche) männlich weiblich<br>(underline) Male Female |
| Alter*<br>Age | *Zwanzig*<br>*Twenty years old* |
| Nationalität*<br>Nationality | *Deutsch*<br>*German* |
| Familienstand<br>Family status | *(unterstreiche) ledig verheiratet*<br>*(underline) single married* |
| Addresse*<br>Address | *Nelkenstraße 11 Bremerhaven. Deutschland*<br>*Nelkenstraße 11, Bremerhaven* |
| Ausbildung<br>Education | *Ich studiere Journalismus im dritten Jahr an der Universität*<br>*I am studying Journalism in the third year at a college* |
| Wo haben Sie zuvor gearbeitet?<br>Where have you worked before? | *Ich habe zwei Monate auf einem Bauernhof gearbeitet*<br>*I worked for two months as a farm worker* |
| Welche Erfahrung und Fähigkeiten haben Sie?<br>What experience and skills have you had? | *Ich kann Auto und Lastwagen fahren und mit dem Computer arbeiten.*<br>*I can drive a car, a truck and I can use a computer* |
| Sprachen*<br>0 - nein, 10 - fließend<br>Languages | *Deutsch - 10, Englisch - 8* |

| | |
|---|---|
| 0 - no, 10 - fluently | *German - 10, English - 8* |
| Führerschein*<br>Driving license | (unterstreiche) *Nein <u>Ja</u> Typ: BC Kann Lastwagen fahren.*<br>*(underline) No <u>Yes</u> Kind: BC, I can drive trucks* |
| Sie brauchen einen Job *<br>You need a job | *(unterstreiche) Vollzeit <u>Teilzeit</u>: 15 Stunden die Woche*<br>*(underline) Full time <u>Part time:</u> 15 hours a week* |
| Sie wollen verdienen<br>You want to earn | *15 Euro die Stunde*<br>*15 euros per hour* |

| **Persönliche Angaben**<br>*Alle mit einem Sternchen * markierten Felder müssen ausgefüllt werden. Die anderen Felder können leer gelassen werden.* | **Personal information form**<br>*You must fill up fields with asterisk *. You can leave other fields blank.* |
|---|---|
| Vorname*<br>First name | *Mike*<br>*Mike* |
| Zweiter Name<br>Middle name | |
| Nachname*<br>Last name | *Sullivan*<br>*Sullivan* |
| Geschlecht*<br>Sex | (unterstreiche) <u>männlich</u> weiblich<br>(underline) <u>Male</u> Female |
| Alter*<br>Age | *einundzwanzig*<br>*Twenty-one years old* |
| Nationalität*<br>Nationality | *US-Amerikaner*<br>*American* |
| Familienstand<br>Family status | *(unterstreiche) <u>ledig</u> verheiratet*<br>*(underline) <u>Single</u> Married* |
| Addresse*<br><br>Address | *Zimer 218, Studentenwohnheim, An der Allee 36, Bremerhaven, Deutschland*<br>*Room 218, student dorms, An der Allee 36, Bremerhaven Germany.* |
| Ausbildung<br>Education | *Ich studiere Computerdesign im zweiten Jahr an der Universität*<br>*I study computer design in the second year at a college* |
| Wo haben Sie zuvor gearbeitet?<br>Where have you worked before? | *Ich habe zwei Monate auf einem Bauernhof gearbeitet*<br>*I worked for two months as a farm worker* |
| Welche Erfahrung und Fähigkeiten haben Sie?<br>What experience and skills have you had? | *Ich kann mit dem Computer umgehen*<br><br>*I can use a computer* |
| Sprachen*<br>0 - nein, 10 - fließend<br>Languages | *Deutsch - 8, Englisch - 10* |

| | |
|---|---|
| 0 - no, 10 - fluently | *German - 8, English - 10,* |
| Führerschein*<br>Driving license | (unterstreiche*) <u>Nein</u> Ja Typ:*<br>*(underline) <u>No</u> Yes Kind:* |
| Sie brauchen einen Job *<br>You need a job | *(unterstreiche) Vollzeit <u>Teilzeit</u>: 15 Stunden die Woche*<br>*(underline) Full time <u>Part time:</u> 15 hours a week* |
| Sie wollen verdienen<br>You want to earn | *15 Euro die Stunde*<br>*15 euros per hour* |

Frau Krämer brachte die Formulare mit ihren persönlichen Angaben zum Herausgeber der „Bremerhavener Nachrichten".

*Miss Krämer took their personal information forms to the editor of "Bremerhavener Nachrichten".*

„Der Herausgeber ist einverstanden", sagte Frau Krämer, als sie zurückkam. „Ihr begleitet eine Polizeistreife und schreibt dann Berichte für die Kriminalrubrik. Morgen um 17 Uhr werdet ihr von einem Polizeiauto abgeholt. Seid pünktlich da, ok?"

*"The editor has agreed," Miss Krämer said when she came back. "You will accompany a police patrol and then compose reports for the criminal rubric. A police car will come tomorrow at seventeen o'clock to take you. Be here at this time, will you?"*

„Klar", antwortete Mike.

*"Sure," Mike answered.*

„Ja, wir werden pünktlich sein", sagte Stefan. „Auf Wiedersehen."

*"Yes, we will," Stefan said. "Goodbye."*

„Auf Wiedersehen", antwortete Frau Krämer.

*"Goodbye," Miss Krämer answered.*

# 27

## Die Polizeistreife (Teil 1)

*The police patrol (part 1)*

## A

**Vokabeln**

1. der Alarm - alarm
2. alle - everybody
3. ängstlich - afraid
4. anschnallen - fasten
5. begleitet - accompanied
6. die Begrenzung - limit
7. bellte - barked
8. der Dieb - thief,
   die Diebe - thieves
9. der Diebstahl - robbery
10. fuhr - drove
11. fuhr los - started (to drive)
12. gerufen - cried
13. geschlossen - closed
14. die Geschwindigkeit - speed
15. getroffen, kennengelernt - met
16. die Handschellen - handcuffs
17. heulend - howling
18. hoch - high
19. hundert - hundred
20. das Mikrofon - microphone
21. öffnete - opened
22. der Polizist - officer, policeman
23. der Polizeihauptmeister - sergeant
24. der Preis - price

25. rasen - to speed
der Raser - speeder
26. raste - rushed
27. der Schlüssel - key
28. der Sicherheitsgurt - seat belts
29. die Sirene - siren
30. tat - did
31. trat - stepped
32. trocknen - to dry,
trocken - dry (adj)
33. sich umsehen - to look around
34. verdammt - damn
35. die Verfolgung - pursuit
36. versuchte - tried
37. verstanden - understood
38. versteckte - hid
39. die Waffe - gun
40. wartete - waited
41. Was ist los? - What is the matter?
42. zeigte - showed
43. zwölf - twelve

## B

### Die Polizeistreife (Teil 1)

Am nächsten Tagen kamen Mike und Stefan um siebzehn Uhr zum Gebäude der Zeitung „Bremerhavener Nachrichten". Das Polizeiauto wartete schon auf sie. Ein Polizist stieg aus dem Auto aus.

„Hallo. Ich bin Polizeihauptmeister Frank Stein", sagte er, als Stefan und Mike zum Auto kamen.

„Hallo, schön, Sie kennenzulernen. Ich heiße Mike. Wir sollen Sie heute begleiten", antwortete Mike.

„Hallo, ich bin Stefan. Haben Sie schon lange auf uns gewartet?", fragte Stefan.

„Nein, ich bin gerade erst gekommen. Lasst uns einsteigen. Wir fangen jetzt mit der Streife in der Stadt an", sagte der Polizist. Sie stiegen alles ins Polizeiauto.

„Begleitet ihr zum ersten Mal eine Polizeistreife", fragte Polizeihauptmeister Stein und machte den Motor an.

„Wir haben noch nie eine Polizeistreife begleitet",

### *The police patrol (part 1)*

*Mike and Stefan arrived at the building of the newspaper "Bremerhavener Nachrichten" at seventeen o'clock next day. The police car was waiting for them already. A policeman got out of the car.*

*"Hello. I am sergeant Frank Stein," he said when Stefan and Mike came to the car.*

*"Hello. Glad to meet you. My name is Mike. We must accompany you," Mike answered.*

*"Hello. I am Stefan. Were you waiting long for us?" Stefan asked.*

*"No. I have just arrived here. Let us get into the car. We begin city patrolling now," the policeman said. They all got into the police car.*

*"Are you accompanying a police patrol for the first time?" sergeant Stein asked starting the engine.*

*"We have never accompanied a police*

antwortete Stefan.

*patrol before," Stefan answered.*

In diesem Moment meldete sich der Polizeifunk: „Achtung P11 und P07! Ein blaues Auto fährt zu schnell auf der Universitätsstraße."

*At this moment the police radio began to talk: "Attention P11 and P07! A blue car is speeding along College street."*

„P07 ist dran", sagte Polizeihauptmeister Stein ins Mikrofon. Dann sagte er zu den Jungs: „Die Nummer unseres Autos ist P07." Ein großes blaues Auto raste mit hoher Geschwindigkeit an ihnen vorbei. Frank Stein nahm das Mikrofon und sagte: „Hier spricht P07. Ich sehe das rasende Auto. Nehme die Verfolgung auf." Dann sagte er zu den Jungs: „Bitte anschnallen!"

*"P07 got it," sergeant Stein said in the microphone. Then he said to the boys: "The number of our car is P07." A big blue car rushed past them with very high speed. Frank Stein took the mic again and said: "P07 is speaking. I see the speeding blue car. Begin pursuit," then he said to the boys: "Fasten your seat belts."*

Das Polizeiauto fuhr schnell los. Der Polizeihauptmeister trat das Gaspedal voll durch und machte die Sirene an. Mit heulender Sirene rasten sie an Gebäuden, Autos und Bussen vorbei. Frank Stein brachte das blaue Auto zum Anhalten. Der Polizeihauptmeister stieg aus dem Auto aus und ging zu dem Raser. Stefan und Mike gingen ihm nach.

*The police car started quickly. The sergeant stepped on the gas up to the stop and switched on the siren. They rushed with the howling siren past buildings, cars and buses. Frank Stein made the blue car stop. Sergeant got out of the car and went to the speeder. Stefan and Mike went after him.*

„Ich bin Polizeibeamter Frank Stein. Zeigen Sie mir bitte Ihren Führerschein", sagte der Polizist zu dem Raser.

*"I am police officer Frank Stein. Show your driving license, please," the policeman said to the speeder.*

„Hier ist mein Führerschein", der Fahrer zeigte seinen Führerschein. „Was ist los?", fragte er wütend.

*"Here is my driving license," the driver showed his driving license. "What is the matter he said angryly.*

„Sie sind mit hundertzwanzig km/h durch die Stadt gefahren. Die Geschwindigkeitsbegrenzung ist fünfzig", sagte der Polizeihauptmeister.

*"You were driving through the city with a speed of one hundred and twenty kilometers an hour. The speed limit is fiftty," the sergeant said.*

„Ach so, das. Wissen Sie, ich habe gerade mein Auto gewaschen. Ich bin ein bisschen schneller gefahren, damit es trocknet", sagte der Mann mit einem schlauen Grinsen.

*"Ah, this. You see, I have just washed my car. So I was driving a little faster to dry it up," the man said with a sly smile.*

„Ist es teuer, Ihr Auto zu waschen?", fragte der Polizist.

*"Does it cost much to wash the car?" the policeman asked.*

„Nein. Es kostet zwölf Euro", sagte der Raser.

*"Not much. It cost twelve euros," the speeder said.*

„Sie kennen die Preise nicht", sagte Polizeihauptmeister Stein. „In Wirklichkeit kostet es Sie zweihundertzwölf Euro, denn Sie werden zweihundert Euro fürs Trocknen zahlen. Hier ist

*"You do not know the prices," sergeant Stein said. "It really costs you two hundred and twelve euros because you will pay two hundred euros for drying the car. Here is*

der Strafzettel. Einen schönen Tag noch", sagte der Polizist. Er gab dem Raser einen Strafzettel für Geschwindigkeitsüberschreitung über zweihundert Euro und seinen Führerschein und ging zurück zum Polizeiauto.

*the ticket. Have a nice day," the policeman said. He gave a speeding ticket for two hundred euros and the driving license to the speeder and went back to the police car.*

„Frank, du hast viel Erfahrung mit Rasern, nicht wahr?", fragte Stefan den Polizisten.

*"Frank, I think you have lots of experiences with speeders, haven't you?" Stefan asked the policeman.*

„Ich habe schon viele kennengelernt", sagte Frank und machte den Motor an. „Zu erst sehen sie wie wütende Tiger oder schlaue Füchse aus. Aber nachdem ich mit ihnen gesprochen habe, sehen sie wie ängstliche Kätzchen oder dumme Affen aus. Wie der im blauen Auto."

*"I have met many of them," Frank said starting the engine. "At first they look like angry tigers or sly foxes. But after I speak with them, they look like afraid kittens or silly monkeys. Like that one in the blue car."*

In der Zwischenzeit fuhr ein kleines, weißes Auto nicht weit vom Stadtpark langsam die Straße entlang. Das Auto hielt in der Nähe eines Ladens. Ein Mann und eine Frau stiegen aus und gingen zu dem Laden. Er war geschlossen. Der Mann sah sich um. Dann holte er schnell einige Schlüssel hervor und versuchte, die Tür zu öffnen. Schließlich öffnete er sie und sie gingen hinein.

*Meanwhile a little white car was slowly driving along a street not far from the city park. The car stopped near a shop. A man and a woman got out of the car and went up to the shop. It was closed. The man looked around. Then he quickly took out some keys and tried to open the door. At last he opened it and they went inside.*

„Schau, so viele Kleider", sagte die Frau. Sie holte eine große Tasche hervor und begann, alles hineinzupacken. Als die Tasche voll war, brachte sie sie zum Auto und kam zurück.

*"Look! There are so many dresses here!" the woman said. She took out a big bag and began to put in everything there. When the bag was full, she took it to the car and came back.*

„Nimm schnell alles! Oh! Was für ein schöner Hut!", sagte der Mann. Er nahm einen großen schwarzen Hut aus dem Schaufenster und zog ihn auf.

*"Take everything quickly! Oh! What a wonderful hat!" the man said. He took from the shop window a big black hat and put it on.*

„Schau dir dieses rote Kleid an! Das finde ich toll!", sagte die Frau und zog schnell das rote Kleid an. Sie hatte keine Taschen mehr. Deswegen nahm sie mehr Sachen in die Hände, rannte nach draußen und packte sie ins Auto. Dann rannte sie nach drinnen, um noch mehr Dinge zu holen.

*"Look at this red dress! I like it so much!" the woman said and quickly put on the red dress. She did not have more bags. So she took more things in her hands, ran outside and put them on the car. Then she ran inside to bring more things.*

Das Polizeiauto P07 fuhr gerade langsam den Stadtpark entlang, als sich der Funk meldete: „Achtung, alle Einheiten. Wir haben einen Einbruchsalarm aus einem Laden in der Nähe des Stadtparks. Die Adresse des Ladens ist Parkstraße 72."

*The police car P07 was slowly driving along the city park when the radio began to talk: "Attention all patrols. We have got a robbery alarm from a shop near the city park. The address of the shop is 72 Park street."*

„P07 ist dran", sagte Frank ins Mikro. „Ich bin ganz in der Nähe. Fahre dorthin." Sie hatten den Laden schnell gefunden und fuhren zu dem weißen Auto. Dann stiegen sie aus dem Auto aus und versteckten sich dahinter. Die Frau im roten Kleid kam aus dem Laden gerannt. Sie legte einige Kleider auf das Polizeiauto und rannte zurück in den Laden. Die Frau tat das sehr schnell. Sie sah nicht, dass es ein Polizeiauto war.

*"P07 got it," Frank said in the mic. "I am very close to this place. Drive there." They found the shop very quickly and drove up to the white car. Then they got out of the car and hid behind it. The woman in new red dress ran out of the shop. She put some dresses on the police car and ran back in the shop. The woman did it very quickly. She did not see that it was a police car!*

„Verdammt! Ich habe meine Waffe auf der Polizeiwache vergessen!", sagte Frank. Mike und Stefan sahen Polizeihauptmeister Stein und dann einander überrascht an. Der Polizist war so verwirrt, dass Stefan und Mike verstanden, dass er Hilfe brauchte. Die Frau rannte wieder aus dem Laden, legte Kleider auf das Polizeiauto und rannte zurück. Dann sagte Stefan zu Frank: „Wir können so tun, als ob wir Waffen haben."

*"Damn it! I forgot my gun in the police station!" Frank said. Mike and Stefan looked at the sergeant Stein and then surprised at each other. The policeman was so confused that Stefan and Mike understood they must help him. The woman ran out of the shop again, put some dresses on the police car and ran back. Then Stefan said to Frank: "We can pretend that we have guns."*

„Lasst uns das machen", antwortete Frank. „Aber ihr steht nicht auf. Die Diebe haben vielleicht Waffen", sagte er und rief dann: „Hier spricht die Polizei! Alle, die im Laden sind, heben ihre Hände und kommen langsam einer nach dem anderen aus dem Laden!"

*"Let's do it," Frank answered. "But you do not get up. The thieves may have guns," he said and then cried. "This is the police speaking! Everybody who is inside the shop put your hands up and come slowly one by one out of the shop!"*

Sie warteten eine Minute. Niemand kam. Dann hatte Mike eine Idee.

*They waited for a minute. Nobody came out. Then Mike had an idea.*

„Wenn ihr nicht rauskommt, hetzen wir den Polizeihund auf euch!", rief er und bellte wie ein großer, wütender Hund. Die Diebe kamen sofort mit erhobenen Händen herausgerannt. Frank legte ihnen schnell Handschellen an und brachte sie ins Polizeiauto. Dann sagte er zu Mike: „Das war eine gute Idee, so zu tun, als ob wir einen Hund hätten. Weißt du, ich habe meine Waffe schon zweimal vergessen. Wenn sie herausfinden, dass ich sie zum dritten Mal vergessen habe, feuern sie mich vielleicht oder lassen mich Büroarbeit machen. Ihr erzählt es doch niemandem, oder?"

*"If you will not come out now, we will set the police dog on you!" he cried and then barked like a big angry dog. The thieves ran out with hands up immediately. Frank quickly put handcuffs on them and got them to the police car. Then he said to Mike: "It was a great idea pretending that we have a dog! You see, I have forgotten my gun two times already. If they learn that I have forgotten it for the third time, they may fire me or make me do office work. You will not tell anybody about it, will you?"*

„Natürlich nicht!", sagte Mike.

*"Sure, not!" Mike said.*

„Nie", sagte Stefan.

*"Never," Stefan said.*

„Vielen dank für eure Hilfe, Jungs!“, Frank schüttelte ihnen herzlich die Hand.

*"Thank you very much for helping me, guys!" Frank shook their hands strongly.*

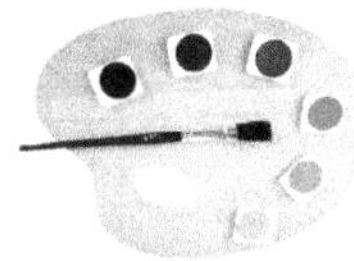

# 28

## Die Polizeistreife (Teil 2)

*The police patrol (part 2)*

 A

**Vokabeln**

1. abprallen - ricochet
2. auch - either, too, also
3. das Bargeld - cash
4. beschützen - to protect
5. bewusstlos - unconscious
6. der Dieb - robber
7. drehte - turned
8. drücken - to press
9. das Einkaufszentrum - shopping center
10. sich entschuldigen - to excuse
    Entschuldigen Sie. - Excuse me.
11. geantwortet - answered
12. gebracht - taken
13. geöffnet - opened

14. gestern - yesterday
15. gestohlen - stolen
16. gewöhnlich - usual
17. das Glas - glass
18. das Handy - mobile
19. heimlich - secretly
20. hochachtungsvoll - yours sincerely
21. jemand - somebody
22. die Kasse - cash register,
    der Kassierer - cashier, teller
23. klingelte - rang
24. der Knopf - button
25. die Männer - men
26. mein - mine
27. noch - yet
28. sahen - saw
29. schlau - clever
30. schoss; angeschossen - shot
31. selten - seldom
32. die Tasche - pocket
33. das Telefon - phone,
    anrufen - to phone
34. der Tresor - safe
35. der Überfall - robbery
36. weg - gone
37. wessen - whose

## B

**Die Polizeistreife (Teil 2)**

Am nächsten Tag begleiteten Mike und Stefan Frank wieder. Sie standen neben einem großen Einkaufszentrum, als eine Frau zu ihnen kam.

„Können Sie mir bitte helfen?“, fragte sie.

„Natürlich. Was ist passiert?“, fragte Frank.

„Mein Handy ist weg. Ich glaube, es wurde gestohlen.“

„Haben Sie es heute schon benutzt?“, fragte der Polizist.

„Ich habe es benutzt, bevor ich das Einkaufszentrum verlassen habe“, antwortete die Frau.

„Lasst uns reingehen“, sagte Frank. Sie gingen ins Einkaufszentrum und sahen sich um. Viele Leute waren da.

„Lasst uns einen alten Trick versuchen“, sagte

***The police patrol (part 2)***

*Next day Mike and Stefan were accompanying Frank again. They were standing near a big shopping centre when a woman came to them.*

*"Can you help me please?" she asked.*

*"Sure, madam. What has happened?" Frank asked.*

*"My mobile phone is gone. I think it has been stolen."*

*"Has it been used today?" the policeman asked.*

*"It had been used by me before I went out of the shopping centre," she answered.*

*"Let's get inside," Frank said. They went into the shopping centre and looked around. There were many people there.*

Frank und holte sein eigenes Handy hervor. „Wie ist Ihre Nummer?“, fragte er die Frau. Sie sagte sie ihm und er wählte sie. Nicht weit von ihnen klingelte ein Handy. Sie gingen zu der Stelle, an der es klingelte. Dort war eine Schlange. Ein Mann in der Schlange sah den Polizisten an und schaute dann schnell weg. Der Polizist ging näher hin und horchte aufmerksam. Das Handy klingelte in der Tasche des Mannes.

„Entschuldigen Sie“, sagte Frank. Der Mann sah ihn an.

„Entschuldigen Sie, Ihr Handy klingelt“, sagte Frank.

„Wo?“, sagte der Mann.

„Hier, in ihrer Tasche“, sagte Frank.

„Nein, es klingelt nicht“, sagte der Mann.

„Doch, es klingelt“, sagte Frank.

„Das ist nicht meins“, sagte der Mann.

„Wessen Telefon klingelt dann in Ihrer Tasche?“, fragte Frank.

„Ich weiß es nicht“, antwortete der Mann.

„Zeigen Sie es mir bitte“, sagte Frank und holte das Handy aus der Tasche des Mannes.

„Oh, das ist meins!“, rief die Frau.

„Hier, nehmen Sie Ihr Telefon“, sagte Frank und gab es ihr.

„Darf ich?“, fragte Frank und steckte seine Hand wieder in die Tasche des Mannes. Er holte ein anderes Handy hervor und dann noch eins.

„Gehören die auch nicht Ihnen?“, fragte Frank den Mann.

Der Mann schüttelte den Kopf und schaute weg.

„Was für seltsame Handys!“, rief Frank. „Sie sind ihren Besitzern davongelaufen und in die Tasche dieses Mannes gesprungen! Und jetzt klingeln sie in seiner Tasche, oder nicht?“

*"Let's try an old trick," Frank said taking out his own phone. "What is your telephone number?" he asked the woman. She said and he called her telephone number. A mobile telephone rang not far from them. They went to the place where it was ringing. There was a queue there. A man in the queue looked at the policeman and then quickly turned his head away. The policeman came closer listening carefully. The telephone was ringing in the man's pocket.*

*"Excuse me," Frank said. The man looked at him.*

*"Excuse me, your telephone is ringing," Frank said.*

*"Where?" the man said.*

*"Here, in your pocket," Frank said.*

*"No, it is not," the man said.*

*"Yes, it is," Frank said*

*"It is not mine," the man said.*

*"Then whose telephone is ringing in your pocket?" Frank asked.*

*"I do not know," the man answered.*

*"Let me see, please," Frank said and took the telephone out of the man's pocket.*

*"Oh, it is mine!" the woman cried.*

*"Take your telephone, madam," Frank said giving it to her.*

*"May I, sir?" Frank asked and put his hand in the man's pocket again. He took out another telephone, and then one more.*

*"Are they not yours either?" Frank asked the man.*

*The man shook his head looking away.*

*"What strange telephones!" Frank cried. "They ran away from their owners and jump into the pockets of this man! And now they*

„Ja, das tun sie", sagte der Mann.

„Wie Sie wissen, ist es mein Job, Menschen zu beschützen. Und ich werde Sie vor ihnen beschützen. Steigen Sie in mein Auto und ich bringe Sie an einen Ort, wo kein Telefon in Ihre Tasche springen kann. Wir fahren aufs Revier", sagte der Polizist. Dann nahm er den Mann am Arm und brachte ihn zum Auto.

„Ich mag dumme Verbrecher", sagte Frank Stein grinsend, nachdem sie den Dieb aufs Revier gebracht hatten.

„Hast du schon schlaue getroffen?", fragte Stefan.

„Ja, das habe ich. Aber es passiert selten"; antwortete der Polizist. „Denn es ist sehr schwer, einen schlauen Verbrecher zu fangen."

In der Zwischenzeit betraten zwei Männer die Deutsche Bank. Einer von ihnen stellte sich in der Schlange an. Ein anderer ging zur Kasse und gab dem Kassierer einen Zettel. Der Kassierer nahm den Zettel und las.

„Sehr geehrter Herr,

das ist ein Überfall auf die Deutsche Bank. Geben Sie mir alles Geld. Wenn Sie es nicht tun, werde ich meine Waffe benutzen. Danke.

Hochachtungsvoll,

Robert."

„Ich denke, ich kann Ihnen helfen", sagte der Kassierer, während er heimlich den Alarmknopf drückte. „Aber das Geld wurde gestern von mir im Tresor eingeschlossen. Der Tresor wurde noch nicht geöffnet. Ich werde jemanden bitten, den Tresor zu öffnen und das Geld zu bringen. Okay?"

„Okay. Aber schnell!", antwortete der Dieb.

„Hätten Sie gerne eine Tasse Kaffee, während das Geld in Taschen gepackt wird?", fragte der Kassierer.

„Nein, danke. Nur Geld", antwortete der Dieb.

*are ringing in his pockets, aren't they?"*

*"Yes, they are," the man said.*

*"You know, my job is to protect people. And I will protect you from them. Get in my car and I will bring you to the place where no telephone can jump in your pocket. We go to the police station," the policeman said. Then he took the man by the arm and took him to the police car.*

*"I like silly criminals," Frank Stein smiled after they had taken the thief to the police station.*

*"Have you met smart ones?" Stefan asked.*

*"Yes, I have. But very seldom," the policeman answered. "Because it is very hard to catch a smart criminal."*

*Meanwhile two men came into the Deutsche Bank. One of them took a place in a queue. Another one came up to the cash register and gave a paper to the cashier. The cashier took the paper and read:*

*"Dear Sir,*

*this is a robbery of the Deutsche Bank. Give me all the cash. If you do not, then I will use my gun. Thank you.*

*Sincerely yours,*

*Robert"*

*"I think I can help you," the cashier said pressing secretly the alarm button. "But the money had been locked by me in the safe yesterday. The safe has not been opened yet. I will ask somebody to open the safe and bring the money. Okay?"*

*"Okay! But do it quickly!" the robber answered.*

*"Shall I make you a cup of coffee while the money is being put in bags?" the cashier asked.*

*"No, thank you. Just money," the robber answered.*

Der Funk im Polizeiauto P07 meldete sich: „Achtung, alle Einheiten. Überfallalarm in der Deutschen Bank."

*The radio in the police car P07 began to talk: "Attention all the patrols. We have got a robbery alarm from the Deutsche Bank."*

„P07 ist dran", antwortete Polizeihauptmeister Stein. Er trat aufs Gas und das Auto fuhr schnell los. Als sie an der Bank ankamen, war noch kein anderes Polizeiauto da.

*"P07 got it," sergeant Stein answered. He stepped on the gas up to the stop and the car started quickly. When they drove up to the bank, there was no other police car yet.*

„Das wird ein interessanter Bericht, wenn wir reingehen", sagte Stefan.

*"We will make an interesting report if we go inside," Stefan said.*

„Ihr Jungs macht, was ihr braucht. Ich gehe durch die Hintertür rein", sagte Polizeihauptmeister Stein. Er holte seine Waffe raus und ging schnell zur Hintertür der Bank. Stefan und Mike betraten die Bank durch die Eingangstür. Sie sahen einen Mann in der Nähe der Kasse stehen. Er hatte eine Hand in seiner Tasche und sah sich um. Der Mann, der mit ihm gekommen war, ging aus der Schlange zu ihm.

*"You guys do what you need. And I will come inside through the back door," sergeant Stein said. He took out his gun and went quickly to the back door of the bank. Stefan and Mike came into the bank through the central door. They saw a man standing near the cash register. He put one hand in his pocket and looked around. The man who came with him, stepped away from the queue and came up to him.*

„Wo ist das Geld?", fragte er Robert.

*"Where is the money?" he asked Robert.*

„Hannes, der Kassierer hat gesagt, dass es in Taschen gepackt wird", antwortete der andere Dieb.

*"Hannes, the cashier has said that it is being put in bags," another robber answered.*

„Ich habe es satt, zu warten", sagte Hannes. Er holte seine Waffe hervor und richtete sie auf den Kassierer. „Bringen Sie jetzt alles Geld!", schrie er. Dann ging er in die Mitte des Raums und rief: „Alle herhören! Das ist ein Überfall! Niemand bewegt sich!", In diesem Moment bewegte sich jemand in der Nähe der Kasse. Der Dieb mit der Waffe schoss auf ihn, ohne hinzuschauen. Der andere Dieb fiel auf den Boden und rief: „Hannes! Du Vollidiot! Verdammt! Du hast mich angeschossen!"

*"I am tired of waiting!" Hannes said. He took out a gun and pointed it to the cashier. "Bring all the money now!" the robber cried at the cashier. Then he went to the middle of the room and cried: "Listen all! This is a robbery! Nobody move!" At this moment somebody near the cash register moved. The robber with the gun without looking shot at him. Another robber fell on the floor and cried: "Hannes! You silly monkey! Damn it! You have shot me!"*

„Oh, Robert! Ich habe nicht gesehen, dass du das bist!", sagte Hannes. In diesem Moment rannte der Kassierer schnell nach draußen.

*"Oh, Robert! I did not see that it was you!" Hannes said. At this moment the cashier quickly ran out.*

„Der Kassierer ist weggerannt und das Geld ist noch nicht hierher gebracht worden!", rief Hannes Robert zu. „Die Polizei kann jeden Moment kommen! Was sollen wir machen?"

*"The cashier has run away and the money has not been taken here yet!" Hannes cried to Robert. "The police may arrive soon! What shall we do?"*

„Nimm etwas Großes, zerschlag das Glas und

*"Take something big, break the glass and*

nimm das Geld! Schnell!“, rief Robert. Hannes nahm einen metallenen Stuhl und schlug auf das Glas der Kasse. Natürlich war es kein gewöhnliches Glas und zerbrach nicht. Doch der Stuhl prallte zurück und traf den Dieb am Kopf! Er fiel bewusstlos zu Boden. In diesem Moment kam Polizeihauptmeister Stein hereingerannt und legte den Dieben schnell Handschellen an. Er drehte sich zu Stefan und Mike um.

*take the money. Quickly!" Robert cried. Hannes took a metal chair and hit the glass of the cash register. It was of course not usual glass and it did not break. But the chair went back by ricochet and hit the robber on the head! He fell on the floor unconsciously. At this moment sergeant Stein ran inside and quickly put handcuffs on the robbers. He turned to Stefan and Mike.*

„Hab ich es doch gesagt! Die meisten Verbrecher sind einfach nur dumm!“, sagte er.

*"I did say! Most criminals are just silly!" he said.*

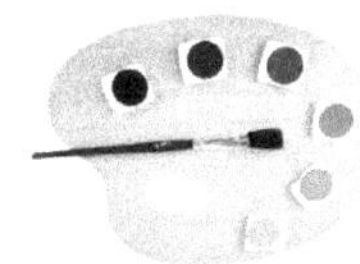

# 29

## Schule für Austauschschüler (SAS) und Au-pair

*School for Foreign Students (SFS) and au pair*

## A

### Vokabeln

1. abgelaufen - passed
2. älter - elder
3. ändern - to change,
   die Änderung - change
4. auch - also
5. die Ausschreibung, der Wettbewerb - competition
6. auswählen, entscheiden für - to choose
   entschied sich für - chose
7. der Bedienstete - servant
8. besuchte - visited
9. bezahlen, zahlen - to pay
   bezahlte, gezahlt - paid

10. der Brief - letter
11. das Datum - date
12. das Dorf - village
13. einmal - once
14. die Email - e-mail
15. der Gastgeber - host
    die Gastfamilie - the host family
16. die Hoffnung - hope,
    hoffen - to hope
17. kommen in - to join
18. der Kurs - course
19. das Land - country
20. lebte - lived
21. lernen - learning
22. die Möglichkeit - possibility
23. nächste - nearest
24. Nordamerika und Eurasien - North America and Eurasia
25. die Person - person
26. das Problem - problem
27. riefen an - called
28. schickte - sent
29. schrieb - wrote
30. seit - since (temporal)
    da, weil - as, since(kausal)
31. standard - standard
32. der Teilnehmer - participant
33. die Tochter - daughter
34. ungerecht - unfair
35. die Vereinbarung - agreement
36. die Vereinigten Staaten, die USA - the United States/the USA
37. die Website - Internet site
38. zweimal - twice

## B

### Schule für Austauschschüler (SAS) und Au-pair

Mikes Schwester, Bruder und Eltern lebten in Amerika. Sie wohnten in Chicago. Seine Schwester hieß Sofia. Sie war zwanzig. Sie lernte Deutsch, seit sie elf war. Als Sofia fünfzehn war, wollte sie an dem Programm SAS teilnehmen. SAS gibt Highschool-Schülern aus den USA und Eurasien die Möglichkeit, ein Jahr in Deutschland zu verbringen, in einer Gastfamilie zu leben und eine deutsche Schule zu besuchen. Das Programm ist kostenlos. Das Flugticket, die Unterkunft in der Familie, Essen und das Besuchen der deutschen Schule werden

### *School for Foreigner Students (SFS) and au pair*

*Mike's sister, brother and parents lived in the United States. They lived in Chicago. The sister's name was Sofia. She was twenty years old. She had learned German since she was eleven years old. When Sofia was fifteen years old, she wanted to take part in the program SFS. SFS gives the possibility for some high school students from North America and Eurasia to spend a year in Germany, living with a host family and studying in a German school. The program is free. Airplane tickets, living with a family, food, studying at German school are paid by*

von SAS gezahlt. Aber als sie sich auf der Website über die Ausschreibung informierte, war die Frist schon abgelaufen.

*SFS. But by the time when she got the information about the competition date from the Internet site, the competition day had passed.*

Dann erfuhr sie von dem Au-pair-Programm. Dieses Programm ermöglicht es den Teilnehmern, ein oder zwei Jahre in einem europäischen Land zu verbringen, bei einer Gastfamilie zu leben, sich um die Kinder zu kümmern und eine Sprachschule zu besuchen. Da Mike gerade in Bremerhaven studierte, schrieb Sofia ihm eine Email. Sie bat ihn darum, eine Gastfamilie für sie in Deutschland zu finden. Mike sah Zeitungen und Webseiten mit Anzeigen durch. Er fand deutsche Gastfamilien auf http://www.aupair-world.net/ und auf http://www.placementaupair.com/. Dann ging Mike zu einer Au-pair-Vermittlung in Bremerhaven. Er wurde von einer Frau beraten. Sie hieß Frauke Stamm.

*Then she learned about the program de au pair. This program gives its participants the possibility to spend a year or two in another country of Europe living with a host family, looking after children and learning at a language course. Since Mike was studying in Bremerhaven, Sofia wrote him an e-mail. She asked him to find a host family for her in Germany. Mike looked through some newspapers and Internet sites with adverts. He found some host families from Germany on http://www.aupair-world.net/ and on http://www.placementaupair.com/. Then Mike visited an au pair agency in Bremerhaven. He was consulted by a woman. Her name was Frauke Stamm.*

„Meine Schwester ist aus den USA. Sie würde gerne als Au-pair bei einer deutschen Familie arbeiten. Können Sie mir helfen?“, fragte Mike Frauke.

*"My sister is from United States. She would like to be an au pair with a German family. Can you help on this matter?" Mike asked Frauke.*

„Natürlich, sehr gerne. Wir vermitteln Au-pairs an Familien in ganz Deutschland. Ein Au-pair kommt in eine Gastfamilie, um im Haus zu helfen und sich um die Kinder zu kümmern. Die Gastfamilie gibt dem Au-pair Essen, ein Zimmer und Taschengeld. Das Taschengeld liegt zwischen 200 und 600 Euro. Die Gastfamilie muss auch einen Sprachkurs für das Aupair bezahlen“, sagte Frauke.

*"I will be glad to help you. We place au pairs with families all over Germany. An au pair is a person who joins a host family to help around the house and look after children. The host family gives the au pair food, a room and pocket money. Pocket money may be from 200 to 600 euros. The host family must pay for a language course for the au pair as well," Frauke said.*

„Gibt es gute und schlechte Familien?“, fragte Mike.

*"Are there good and bad families?" Mike asked.*

„Es gibt zwei Probleme bei der Wahl einer Familie. Zum einen denken manche Familien, dass ein Au-pair ein Bediensteter sei, der alles im Haus machen muss, einschließlich für die ganze Familie kochen, putzen, waschen, Gartenarbeit usw. Aber ein Au-pair ist kein Bediensteter. Ein Au-pair ist wie eine ältere Tochter oder ein älterer Sohn der Familie, der

*"There are two problems about choosing a family. First some families think that an au pair is a servant who must do everything in the house including cooking for all family members, cleaning, washing, working in the garden etc. But an au pair is not a servant. An au pair is like an elder daughter or son of the family who helps parents with younger*

den Eltern mit den jüngeren Kindern hilft. Um ihre Rechte zu schützen, müssen die Au-pairs eine Vereinbarung mit der Gastfamilie ausarbeiten. Glaub bloß nicht, wenn Au-pair-Vermittlungen oder Gastfamilien sagen, dass sie eine Standardvereinbarung verwenden. Es gibt keine Standardvereinbarung. Das Au-pair kann jeden Teil der Vereinbarung ändern, wenn sie ungerecht ist. Alles, was ein Au-pair und die Gastfamilie machen, muss schriftlich in der Vereinbarung festgehalten werden.

*children. To protect their rights au pairs must work out an agreement with the host family. Do not believe it when some au pair agencies or host families say that they use a "standard" agreement. There is no standard agreement. The au pair can change any part of the agreement if it is unfair. Everything that an au pair and host family will do must be written in an agreement.*

Das zweite Problem ist: Manche Familien leben in kleinen Dörfern, in denen es keine Sprachkurse und wenige Orte gibt, wo das Au-pair in seiner Freizeit hingehen kann. In diesem Fall muss die Vereinbarung enthalten, dass die Gastfamilie für Hin- und Rückfahrkarten in die nächste größere Stadt zahlen muss, wenn das Au-pair dorthin fährt. Das kann ein- oder zweimal die Woche sein."

*The second problem is this: Some families live in small villages where there are no language courses and few places where an au pair can go in free time. In this situation it is necessary to include in the agreement that the host family must pay for two way tickets to the nearest big town when the au pair goes there. It may be once or twice a week."*

„Alles klar. Meine Schwester hätte gerne eine Familie aus Bremerhaven. Können Sie eine gute Familie in dieser Stadt finden?", fragte Mike.

*"I see. My sister would like a family from Bremerhaven. Can you find a good family in this city?" Mike asked.*

„Na ja, im Moment haben wir etwa zwanzig Familien aus Bremerhaven", antwortete Frauke. Sie rief ein paar von ihnen an. Die Gastfamilien waren froh, ein Au-pair-Mädchen aus den USA zu bekommen. Die meisten Familien wollten einen Brief mit einem Foto von Sofia. Manche wollten sie auch anrufen, um sicher zu gehen, dass sie ein bisschen Deutsch sprach. Also gab Mike ihnen ihre Telefonnummer.

*"Well, there are about twenty families from Bremerhaven now," Frauke answered. She telephoned some of them. The host families were glad to have an au pair from United States. Most of the families wanted to get a letter with a photograph from Sofia. Some of them also wanted to telephone her to be sure that she can speak German a little. So Mike gave them her telephone number.*

Ein paar Gastfamilien riefen Sofia an. Dann schickte sie ihnen Briefe. Schließlich entschied sie sich für eine passende Familie und arbeitete mit Fraukes Hilfe eine Vereinbarung mit ihnen aus. Die Familie bezahlte das Ticket von den USA nach Deutschland. Schließlich fuhr Sofia voller Hoffnungen und Träume nach Deutschland.

*Some host families called Sofía. Then she sent them letters. At last she chose a suitable family and with the help of Frauke worked out an agreement with them. The family paid for the ticket from United States to Germany. At last Sofia started for Germany full of hopes and dreams.*

## German-English dictionary

Abend der - evening

Abenteuer das - adventure

aber - but

abgelaufen - passed

abgestürzt - fallen

abladen - to unload

ablehnen - to refuse

abprallen - ricochet

acht - eight

achter - eighth

Affe der - monkey

Agentur die - agency

Alarm der - alarm

alle - all, everybody

alles - everything

als - than,
Elmar ist älter als Linda. - Elmar is older than Linda.

älter - elder

Alter das - age

am, beim - at

Amerikaner - American

andere - other

anderer - another

ändern - to change,
die Änderung - change

anfangen - to begin

angekommen - arrived

ängstlich - afraid

anhalten - to stop

ankommen - to arrive, to get (somewhere)

Anrufbeantworter der - answering machine

anrufen - to call on the phone;
rufen - call;
das Callcenter - call centre

anschnallen - fasten

anstelle von - instead of
an deiner Stelle - instead of you

Antwort die - answer,
antworten - to answer

Anzeige die - advert

Apotheke die - pharmacy

Arbeit die - job

arbeitend - working

Arbeiter der - worker

Arbeitgeber der - employer

Arbeitsvermittlung die - job agency

ärgern - to bother

arm - poor

Arm der - arm

Art die - kind, type

Arzt der - doctor

Aspirin das - aspirin

auch - as well, also, either, too

auf - on

Auf Wiedersehen - goodbye

Aufgabe die - task

Aufmerksamkeit die - attention
achten auf - pay attention to

aufnehmen - to record

aufstehen - to get up

Steh auf! - Get up!

Aufzug der - lift

Auge das - eye

Augen die - eyes

aus - from
  aus den USA - from the USA

Ausbildung die - education

ausgeben, verwenden - to spend

ausgestopft - stuffed;
  Fallschirmspringerpuppe - stuffed parachutist

ausgewertet - estimated

Ausschreibung die, Wettbewerb der - competition

außer Betrieb - out of order

Außerirdische der - alien

aussteigen - to get off

auswählen, entscheiden für - to choose
  entschied sich für - chose

Auto das - car

Bad das, Badezimmer das - bathroom;

Badewanne die - bath

Badezimmertisch der - bathroom table

Bahnhof der - railway station

bald - soon

Bank die – bank
  Ich gehe zur Bank. - I go to the bank.

Bargeld das - cash

Bauer der - farmer

Bauernhof der - farm

bedienen - to serve

Bedienstete der - servant

beendete - stopped

befehlen - to order

Begabung die - gift

begann - began

begleiten - to accompany

begleitet - accompanied

Begrenzung die - limit

beibringen - to teach

Bein das - leg

Beispiel das - example;
  zum Beispiel - for example

beißen - to bite

bekommen - to get (possesion of)

beladen - to load,
  der Verlader - loader

bellte - barked

benutzen - to use

beraten - to consult

Berater der - consultant

Beratung die - consultancy

berichten - to report
  der Reporter - reporter

Beruf der - profession

beschützen - to protect

Besitzer der - owner

besser - better

beständig - constant

besuchte - visited

Bett das - bed

Betten die - beds

beurteilen - to estimate

bewegte sich - moved

bewusstlos - unconscious

bezahlen, zahlen - to pay

bezahlte, gezahlt - paid

Billionen - billion

bis - until

bitte - please

bitten, fragen - to ask

blass - pale

Blatt das - sheet (of paper)

blau - blue

bleiben - to remain

Blume die - flower

Boden der - floor

brauchen - need

Bremse die - brake,

bremsen - to brake

Brief der - letter

bringen - to bring

Brot das - bread

Brücke die - bridge

Bruder der - brother

Buch das - book

Bücherregal das - bookcase

Büro das - office

Bus der - bus
mit dem Bus fahren - to go by bus

Butter die - butter

Butterbrot das - sandwich

Café das - café

CD die - CD

CD-Spieler der - CD player

Chance die - chance

Chemie die - chemistry

chemisch - chemical(adj)
die Chemikalien - chemicals

Computer der - computer

da, weil - since, as

Dach das - roof

danken - to thank;

danke - thank you, thanks

dann - then

danach - after that

dass - that (conj)
Ich weiß, dass dieses Buch interessant ist. - I know that this book is interesting.

Datum das - date

dauern - to last, to take
Der Film dauert mehr als 3 Stunden - The movie is more than three hours long

dein - your

denken - to think

der, die, das (Konj.) - which

der/die/das gleiche - the same
gleichzeitig - at the same time

Design das - design

deswegen - so

Deutsche der, Deutsche die - German

Deutschland - Germany

die Adresse - address

Dieb der - thief, robber

Diebe die - thieves

Diebstahl der - robbery

diese (Pl.) - these, those

dieser, diese, dieses - this;

dieses Buch - this book

Ding das, Sache die - thing
diese Dinge - this stuff

Dorf das - village

dort - there

draußen - outdoors

dreckig - dirty

drehen - to turn;
  anmachen - to turn on;
  ausmachen - to turn off

drehte - turned

drei - three

dreißig - thirty

dritter - third

drücken - to press

du - you

du/ihr - you

dumm - silly

dunkel - dark

dürfen, können - may
  nicht dürfen - must not

DVD die - DVD

eigen - own

Eimer der - pail

ein - one

ein paar - some, a pair

einer nach dem anderen - one by one

einer von euch - either of you

einfach - just; simple

einige - some

Einkaufszentrum das - shopping center

einmal - once

einundzwanzig - twenty-one

einverstanden sein - to agree

einzeln - individually

Eis das - ice-cream

elektrisch - electric

elf - eleven

Eltern die - parent

Email die - e-mail

empfehlen - to recommend;
  die Empfehlung - recommendation

empfohlen - recommended

Ende das - finish
  beenden - to finish

Energie die - energy

entlang - along

entwerfen, verfassen - to compose

entwickeln - to develop

Entwurf der, Text der - composition

er - he

er kam, gekommen - came

Erde die - earth

Erfahrung die - experience

erhalten (etwas) - to get (something)

erinnerte sich - remembered

erklären - to explain

ernst - seriously

erst - at first

erstarren - to freeze

erwidern - answer

es - it

essen - to eat

Essen das - food

etwa - about

etwas - something, anything

Fachbuch das - textbook

Fähigkeit die - skill

fahren - to drive
der Fahrer - driver

Fahrkarte die - ticket

Fahrrad das - bike

Fahrrad fahren, mit dem Fahrrad fahren - to go by bike, to ride a bike

fallen - to fall
fiel - fell
der Fall - fall

fallend - falling

Fallschirm der - parachute

Fallschirmspringer der - parachutist

Familie die - family

fangen - to catch

Feier die - ceremony

Feld das - field

Fenster das - window

Fenster die - windows

Fernseher der - TV-set

fertig - finished; ready

Feuer das - fire

feuern - to fire

Film der - film

Finanzwissenschaft die - finance

finden - to find

Firma die - firm

Firmen die - firms

fließend - fluently

flog weg - flew away

Flugschau die - airshow

Flugzeug das - airplane

Fluss der - to flow

Formular das - form

fortführen - to continue;
weiter schauen - continued to watch

Fortsetzung folgt - to be continued

Foto das - picture

fotografieren - to photograph;
der Fotograf - photographer

Fragebogen der - questionnaire

Frau die - woman

Fräulein - Miss

frei - free
die Freizeit, freie Zeit - free time

freisetzen - to set free

fremd - strange

Freund der - friend

Freundin die - girlfriend

freundlich - friendly

froh - glad

Frühstück das - breakfast;
frühstücken - to have breakfast

fuhr - drove

fuhr los - started (to drive)

führen - running

Führer der - leader

Führerschein der - driving license

füllen - to fill up

fünf - five

fünfter - fifth

fünfundzwanzig - twenty-five

fünfzehn - fifteen

für - for

Fuß der - foot
zu Fuß - on foot

füttern - to feed

gab - gave

Garten der - garden

Gas das - gas

Gast der - guest

Gastgeber der - host

geantwortet - answered

gearbeitet - worked

geben - to hand

gebracht - taken

gefallen - to like;

Das gefällt mir. - I like that.

gefragt - asked

Gefühl das - feeling

gefunden - found

gegen - against

Geheimnis das - secret

gehen - to walk

gelb - yellow

Geld das - money

geliebt - loved

Genesung die, Rehabilitation - rehabilitation

geöffnet - opened

gerufen - cried

gesäubert - cleaned

Geschichte die - story

Geschlecht das - sex

geschlossen - closed

Geschwindigkeit die - speed

Gesicht das - face

gestern - yesterday

gestohlen - stolen

gesund pflegen - to rehabilitate

Gesundheit die - health

getroffen, kennengelernt - met

gewöhnlich - usual

Glas das - glass

glauben - to believe
seinen Augen nicht trauen - to not believe one's eyes

Glück das - happiness

glücklich - happy

grau - grey

grauhaarig - grey-headed

groß - big

größer - bigger

groß-größer-am größten - big-bigger-biggest

grün - green

Grund der - reason

Gummi der - rubber

gut - good, well

gut, alles klar - OK, well

Haar das - hair

haben - to have

er/sie/es hat - he/she/it has;
Er hat ein Buch. - He has a book.

halb - half

hallo - hello, hi

Handarbeit die - manual work

Handschellen die - handcuffs

Handy das - mobile

hassen - to hate

hatte - had

Haupt-, zentral - central

Haus das - house

Hausaufgaben die - homework

Haustier das - pet

heimlich - secretly

Helfer der - helper

Herausgeber der - editor

Herr, Hr. - mister, Mr.

herstellen - to produce

heulend - howling

heute - today

Hey! - Hey!

hier (Ort) - here (a place),

hierher (Richtung) - here (a direction),

hier ist - here is

Hilfe die - help;

helfen - to help

hindurch - through

hinter - behind

hoch - high

hochachtungsvoll - yours sincerely

Hof der - yard

Hoffnung die - hope,
hoffen - to hope

hören - to listen;
Ich höre Musik. - I listen to music.

hörte - heard

Hose die - trousers

Hotel das - hotel

Hotels die - hotels

Hund der - dog

hundert - hundred

hungrig - hungry
Ich habe Hunger. - I am hungry.

Hut der - hat

ich - I

Idee die - idea

ihm - him

ihr - their

ihr Buch - her book

Imbiss der - snack

immer - always

in - in

in - inside

in - into

in der Zwischenzeit - meanwhile

Information die, Angabe die - information

informieren, mitteilen - to inform

informierte - informed

Ingenieur der - engineer

Inserat das - ad

intelligent - smart

interessant - interesting

irgendwelche - any

ja - yes

Jacke die - jacket

Jahr das - year

Jahreszeit die - season

jeder, jede, jedes - every

jemand - somebody

jener, jene, jenes - that

jetzt, zurzeit, gerade - now

Journalist der - journalist

jung - young

Junge der - boy, guy

Kabel das - cable

Kaffee der - coffee

kalt - cold (adj)

die Kälte - coldness

Känguru das - kangaroo

Kapitän der - captain

Karte die - map

Kasse die - cash register,

Kassierer der - cashier, teller

Kätzchen das - kitten

Katze die - cat

kaufen - to buy

kennen - to know

kennengelernt - learned about

Kessel der - kettle

Kilometer der - kilometer

Kind das - child

Kinder die - children

Kindergarten der - kindergarten

Kiste die - box

klar, sicher - sure

Klasse die - class

Klassenzimmer das - classroom

Kleidung die - clothes

klein - little, small

klingeln - to ring,
das Klingeln - ring

klingelte - rang

Knopf der - button

Koch der / Köchin die - cooker

kochend - cooking

Kollege der - colleague

kommen - come, go

kommen in - to join

können - can
Ich kann lesen. - I can read.

könnte - could

Kontrolle die - control

kontrollieren - to check

Koordination die - co-ordination

Kopf der - head;
gehen - to head, to go

Kopfarbeit die - mental work

kosten - to cost

kreativ - creative

Krieg der - war

Kristal das - crystal

Krug der - jar

Küche die - kitchen

Kunde der - customer

Kunst die - art

Künstler der - artist

Kurs der - course

kurz - short

küssen - to kiss

Küste die - seashore

Küste die - shore

Lächeln das - smile

lächeln - to smile

lächelte - smiled

lachen - to laugh

laden - to load

Laden der - shop

Läden die - shops

Land das - country

landen - to land

lang- long

langsam - slowly

Laser der - laser

lass uns - let us

lassen - to let

Lastwagen der - truck

laufen - walking

laut - aloud

Leben das - life,
Rettungstrick - life-saving trick

leben, wohnen - to live

lebte - lived

lecker - tasty

ledig - single

leer - blank, empty

legen - to place

Lehrer der - teacher

leicht - slightly

leid tun - to be sorry
Es tut mir leid. - I am sorry.

leise - silent, silently

Lektion die - lesson

lenken - to steer

lernen - to learn

lesen - to read

lesend - reading

liebe - dear

Liebe die - love,

lieben - to love

Lieblings- - favourite
der Lieblingsfilm - favourite film

links - left

Liste die - list

Lösung die - solution, answer

Löwe der - lion

Luft die - air

lustig - funny

machen - to make, to do
die Kaffeemaschine - coffee-maker

machte an - switched on

Mädchen das - girl

Mama, die Mutter - mom, mother

manchmal, ab und zu - sometimes

Mann der - man

männlich - male

Mannschaft die - team

Maschine die - machine

Matratze die - mattress

medizinisch - medical

Meer das - sea

mehr - more

mein, meine, mein - my

Mensch der - human

Menschen die - people

Metall das - metal

Meter der - meter

Methode die - method

mich - me

Miezekatze die - pussycat

Mikrofon das - microphone

Minute die - minute

mit - with

Mitglied das - member

Möbel die - furniture

mögen, lieben - to like, to love

möglich - possible

so oft wie möglich - as often as possible

Möglichkeit die - possibility

Moment der - moment

monoton - monotonous

Montag - Monday

Mörder der - killer

morgen - tomorrow

Morgen der - morning

Motor der - engine

müde - tired

Musik die - music

müssen - must
Ich muss gehen. - I must go.

Mutter die - mother

Muttersprache die - native language

nach - after

nach - past;
um halb neun - at half past eight

nach unten - down

Nachbar der - neighbour

nächste - nearest

Nacht die - night

nahe - close

Nähe die - nearness
in der Nähe - near, nearby, next

näher - closer

nahm - took

Name der - name;
nennen - to name

Nase die - nose

nass - wet

Nationalität die - nationality

Natur die - nature

natürlich - of course

nehmen - to take

nein - no

neu - new

neun - nine

neunter - ninth

nicht - not

nichts - nothing

nie - never

niemand - nobody

noch - yet

noch einen - one more

noch, weiterhin - still

Nordamerika und Eurasien - North America and Eurasia

normal - usual

normalerweise - usually

Notiz die - note

Notizbuch das - notebook

Notizbücher die - notebooks

Nummer die - number

nur - only

ob - if

obwohl, trotzdem - although

öffnen - to open

öffnete - opened

oft - often

Oh! - Oh!

ohne - without
  wortlos - without a word

Ohr das - ear

okay, gut - okay, well

Öl das - oil

Panik die - panic
  in Panik versetzen - to panic

Papa - daddy

Papier das - paper

Park der - park

Parks die - parks

passend - suitable

passieren - to happen,

passiert - happened

Patroiulle die, Streife die - patrol

Pause die - break, pause

Person die - person

Personalabteilung die - personnel department

persönlich - personal

Piepton der - beep

Pilot der - pilot

Plan der - plan

planen - to plan

Planet der - planet

Platz der - square

plötzlich - suddenly

Polen - Poland

Polizei die - police

Polizeihauptmeister der - sergeant

Polizist der - officer, policeman

Position die - position

Preis der - price

pro Stunde - per hour

Problem das - problem

Programm das - program

Programmierer der - programmer

Prüfung die - test

prüfen - to test
  eine Prüfung bestehen - to pass a test

Publikum das - audience

Puppe die - doll

putzen - to wash

Rad das - wheel

Radar der - radar

Radio das - radio

rasen - to speed
  der Raser - speeder

raste - rushed

Rätsel das - mystery

Ratte die - rat

Raumschiff das - spaceship

rechts - right

Rede die - speech

Regel die - rule

Regen der - rain

reiben - to rub

reisen - to travel

rennen, joggen, laufen - to run

retten - to rescue, to save

Rettungsdienst der - rescue service

richtete - pointed

richtig - correct, correctly
falsch - incorrectly
korrigieren - to correct

riefen an - called

rot - red

Rubrik die - rubric

rund - round

Saatgut das - seed

sagen - to tell, to say

sagte - said

sahen - saw

Samstag der - Saturday

Sand der - sand

Sandwich das - sandwich

Sänger der - singer

Satz der - phrase

sauber - clean

sauber machen, putzen - to clean

schauen, betrachten - to look

schaukeln - to pitch

schaute - looked

schickte - sent

Schiff das - ship

schlafen - to sleep

schlagen - to hit, to beat

Schlange die - queue

schlau - clever, sly

schlau - sly, slyly

schlecht - bad

schließen - to close

schließlich - at last

schlucken, hinunterschlucken - to swallow

Schlüssel der - key

schnell - quick, quickly

schon - already

schön - nice

schoss; angeschossen - shot

schreiben - to write

Schreibtisch der - desk

schrieb - wrote

Schriftsteller der - writer

Schritt der - step,
treten - to step

Schule die - school

schütten - to pour

Schwanz der - tail

schwarz - black

Schweiz die - Switzerland

Schweizer - Swiss

schwer - difficult, hard

Schwester die - sister

schwimmen - to swim

sechs - six

sechster - sixth

sechzig - sixty

See der - lake

sehen - to see

sehr - very

sein - its (for neuter); to be

sein, seine - his;
sein Bett - his bed

seit - since (temporal)
da, weil - as, since(kausal)

Sekretärin die - secretary

selten - seldom

Serie die - serial

setzen - to sit

sich anziehen - to put on
angezogen - dressed

sich bewerben - to apply

sich entschuldigen - to excuse
Entschuldigen Sie. - Excuse me.

sich hinsetzen - to sit down

sich kennen - to know each other

sich kümmern um - to care

sich schämen - to be ashamed;
er schämt sich - he is ashamed

sich Sorgen machen - to worry
Mach dir keinen Kopf! - Do not worry!

sich umsehen - to look around

sich unterhalten - to talk

sich verstecken - to hide

das Versteckspiel - hide-and-seek

Sicherheitsgurt der - seat belts

sie - she; they

sieben - seven

siebter - seventh

siebzehn - seventeen (hour)

singen - sing

Sirene die - siren

Situation die - situation

Sitz der - seat,
sich hinsetzen - to take a seat

sofort - immediately

Sohn der - son

sorgfältig - careful

Spaniel der - spaniel

spanisch - Spanish

Spaß der - fun

Spaß haben, genießen - enjoy

spielen - to play

Spielzeug das - toy

Sport der - sport;

Sportgeschäft das - sport shop,

Sportfahrrad das - sport bike

Sprache die - language

sprechen - to speak

springen - to jump;

der Sprung - jump

Stadt die - city, town

Stand der - status,
Familienstand der - family status

standard - standard

stark - strong, strongly

Stärke die - strength

stattdessen - instead

Stechmücke die - mosquito

Stefans Buch - Stefan's book

stehen - to stand

stehlen - to steal

Stein der - stone

sterben - to die,
starb - died

Stern der - star

Sternchen das - asterisk

Stift der - pen

Stifte die - pens

Stimme die - voice

stinkend - stinking

stoßen, ziehen - to push

Straße die - road

Straße die - street

Straßen die - streets

Strom der - current

Student der - student

Studenten die - students

Studentenwohnheim das - dorms

studieren - to study

Stuhl der - chair

Stunde die - hour

stündlich - hourly

super, toll - great

Supermarkt der - supermarket

Tablette die - pill

Tag der - day

Tag der - day

täglich, jeden Tag - daily

Tanker der - tanker

tanzen - to dance;
getanzt (Part.) - danced

tanzend - dancing

Tasche die - bag, pocket

Tasse die - cup

Tastatur die - keyboard

tat - did

tausend - thousand

Taxi das - taxi

Taxifahrer der - taxi driver

Tee der - tea

Teil der - part

teilnehmen - to take part

Teilnehmer der - participant

Telefon das - telephone;
telefonieren - to telephone

Telefonhörer der - phone handset

Teller der - plate

Text der - text

Tier das - animal

Tierarzt der - vet

Tiger der - tiger

Tisch der - table

Tische die - tables

Tochter die - daughter

tödlich - deadly

Toilette die - toilet

tötete, getötet (Part.) - killed

trainieren - to train

trainiert - trained

Transport der - transport

trat - stepped

Traum der - dream,

träumen - to dream

traurig - sad

treffen, kennenlernen - to meet

treiben - floating, to float

Treppe die - stairs

Tresor der - safe

treten - to step

Trick der - trick

trinken - to drink

trocknen - to dry,

trocken - dry (adj)

tschüss - bye

Tür die - door

über - over, across

Überfall der - robbery

übergreifen - to spread

Überraschung die - surprise

überraschen - to surprise

überrascht, verwundert - surprised

Übersetzer der - translator

übrigens - by the way

Uhr - o'clock
  Es ist zwei Uhr. - It is two o'clock.

Uhr die - watch

um eins - at one o'clock

und - and

Unfall der - accident

ungerecht - unfair

Universität die, Uni die - college

uns - us

unser - our

unter - under

unterstreichen - to underline

usw. - etc.

Vater der - dad

Verbrecher der - criminal

verdammt - damn

verdienen - to earn
  Ich verdiene 10 Euro pro Stunde - I earn 10 euros per hour.

Verein der - club

Vereinbarung die - agreement

Vereinigten Staaten die, USA die - the United States/the USA

Verfolgung die - pursuit

vergessen - to forget

verkaufen - to sell

Verkäufer der, Verkäuferin die - shop assistant

Verlag der - publishing

verlassen - to leave

verlieren - to loose

verschieden - different

verstanden - understood

versteckte - hid

verstehen - to understand

versuchen - to try

versuchte - tried

verwirrt - confused

Videokassette die - videocassette

Videothek die - video-shop

viel - many, much *uncount.*

viel zu tun haben - to have a lot of work

viele - much, many *count.*

vielseitig, alles könnend - all-round

vier - four

vierte - fourth

vierundvierzig - forty-four

Vogel der - bird

voll - full

vor - before; ago

vor einem Jahr - a year ago

vor allem - especially

vorbei - past

vorbereiten - to prepare

vorgeben; so tun, als ob - to pretend

vorne - front
  die Vorderräder - front wheels

vorsichtig - carefully
  genau zuhören - to listen carefully

wackelte - shook

Waffe die - gun

wählen, aussuchen - to choose

während - while

Wal der - whale,
  Schwertwal der - killer whale

war - was

waren - were

warm - warm;
  aufwärmen - to warm up

warten - to wait

wartete - waited

was - what

Was ist das? - What is this?
  Welcher Tisch? - What table?

Was ist los? - What is the matter?

waschen - to wash

Waschmaschine die - washer

Wasser das - water

Wasserhahn der - tap

Website die - Internet site

weg - away

Weg der - way

weggehen - to go away

weglaufen - run away

weiblich - female

weil - because

weinen, schreien, rufen - to cry

weiß - white

weit - far

weiter - further

Welle die - wave

Welpe der - puppy

Welt die - world

Weltall das - space

weniger - less

wenigstens - at least

wenn - when

wer - who

Werbung die - advert

werden - will

wessen - whose

Wetter das - weather

wichtig - important

wie - as

wie - how

wieder - again

Wind der - wind

wir - we

wirklich - real, really

wo - where

Woche die - week

wohnhaft - living

wollen - to want

wollte - wanted

Wort das, Vokabel die - word

Wörter die, Vokabeln die - words

wunderbar - wonderful

wunderschön - beautiful

wusste - knew

wütend - angrily, angry

zahlen - to pay

Zebra das - zebra

zehn - ten

zehnter - tenth

zeigen - to show

zeigte - showed

Zeit die - time

Zeitschrift die - magazine

Zeitung die - newspaper

Zentrum das - centre
  Stadtzentrum das - city centre

zerstören - destroy

ziehen - to pull

ziemlich - quite

Zimmer das - room

Zimmer die - rooms

zittern - to shake

Zoo der - zoo

Zug der - train

Zuhause das - home
  nach Hause gehen - go home

zukünftig - future

zurück - back

zusammen - together

zwanzig - twenty

zwei - two

zweimal - twice

zweite Name - middle name

zweiter - second

zwischen - between

zwölf - twelve

## English-German dictionary

about - etwa

accident - der Unfall

accompanied - begleitet

accompany *(v)* - begleiten

across - über

ad - das Inserat

address - die Adresse

adventure - das Abenteuer

advert - die Anzeige, die Werbung

afraid - ängstlich

after - nach

again - wieder

against - gegen

age - das Alter

agency - die Agentur

ago - vor

a year ago - vor einem Jahr

agree *(v)* - einverstanden sein

agreement - die Vereinbarung

air - die Luft

airplane - das Flugzeug

airshow - die Flugschau

alarm - der Alarm

alien - der Außerirdische

all - alle

all-round - vielseitig, alles könnend

along - entlang

aloud - laut

already - schon

also - auch

although - obwohl, trotzdem

always - immer

American - Amerikaner

and - und

angrily - wütend

angry - wütend

animal - das Tier

another - anderer

answer - die Antwort

answer *(v)* - antworten, erwidern

answered - geantwortet

answering machine - der Anrufbeantworter

any - irgendwelche

anything - etwas, nichts

apply *(v)* - sich bewerben

arm - der Arm

arrive *(v)* - ankommen

arrived - angekommen

art - die Kunst

artist - der Künstler

as - da, wie

as well - auch

ask *(v)* - bitten, fragen

asked - gefragt

aspirin - das Aspirin

asterisk - das Sternchen

at - am, beim

at first - erst

at last - schließlich

at least - wenigstens

at one o'clock - um eins

attention - die Aufmerksamkeit
pay attention to - achten auf

audience - das Publikum

away - weg

back - zurück

bad - schlecht

bag - die Tasche

bank - die Bank

I go to the bank. - Ich gehe zur Bank.

barked - bellte

Bathroom - das Bad, das Badezimmer;

bath - die Badewanne

bathroom table - der Badezimmertisch

be - sein

be ashamed; - sich schämen
he is ashamed - er schämt sich

be sorry - leid tun
I am sorry. - Es tut mir leid.

beautiful - wunderschön

because - weil

bed - das Bett

beds - die Betten

beep - der Piepton

before - vor

began - begann

begin *(v)* - anfangen

behind - hinter

believe *(v)* - glauben
to not believe one's eyes - seinen Augen nicht trauen

better - besser

between - zwischen

big - groß

big/bigger/the biggest - groß/größer/am größten

bike - das Fahrrad

billion - Billionen

bird - der Vogel

bite *(v)* - beißen

black - schwarz

blank, empty - leer

blue - blau

book - das Buch

bookcase - das Bücherregal

bother *(v)* - ärgern

box - die Kiste

boy - der Junge

boyfriend - der Freund

brake - die Bremse

brake *(v)* - bremsen

bread - das Brot

break, pause - die Pause

breakfast - das Frühstück
have breakfast - frühstücken

bridge - die Brücke

bring *(v)* - bringen

brother - der Bruder

bus - der Bus
go by bus - mit dem Bus fahren

but - aber

butter - die Butter

button - der Knopf

buy *(v)* - kaufen

by the way - übrigens

bye - tschüss

cable - das Kabel

café - das Café

call on the phone - anrufen

call *(v)* - rufen
  call centre - das Callcenter

called - riefen an

came - kam, gekommen

can - können
  I can read. - Ich kann lesen.

captain - der Kapitän

car - das Auto

care *(v)* - sich kümmern um

careful - sorgfältig

carefully - vorsichtig
  listen carefully - genau zuhören

cash - das Bargeld

cash register - die Kasse

cashier, teller - der Kassierer

cat - die Katze

catch *(v)* - fangen

CD - die CD

CD player - der CD-Spieler

central - haupt-, zentral

centre - das Zentrum
  city centre - das Stadtzentrum

ceremony - die Feier

chair - der Stuhl

chance - die Chance

change *(v)* - ändern

change - die Änderung

check *(v)* - kontrollieren

chemical(adj) - chemisch

chemicals - die Chemikalien

chemistry - die Chemie

child - das Kind

children - die Kinder

choose *(v)* - auswählen, entscheiden für

chose - entschied sich für

city - die Stadt

class - die Klasse

classroom - das Klassenzimmer

clean *(adj)* - sauber

clean *(v)* - sauber machen, putzen

cleaned - gesäubert

clever - schlau

close *(v)* - schließen

close *(adv)* - nah

closed - geschlossen

closer - näher

clothes - die Kleidung

club - der Verein

coffee - der Kaffee

cold (adj) - kalt

coldness - die Kälte

colleague - der Kollege

college - die Universität, die Uni

come, go - kommen

company - die Firma

competition - die Ausschreibung, der Wettbewerb

compose *(v)* - entwerfen, verfassen

composition - der Entwurf, der Text

computer - der Computer

confused - verwirrt

constant - beständig

consult *(v)* - beraten

consultancy - die Beratung

consultant - der Berater

continue *(v)* - fortführen

continued to watch - weiter schauen

control - die Kontrolle

Cooker - der Koch/die Köchin

cooking - kochend

co-ordination - die Koordination

correct, correctly - richtig
incorrectly - falsch

correct *(v)* - korrigieren

cost *(v)* - kosten

could - könnte, kann

country - das Land

course - der Kurs

creative - kreativ

cried - gerufen

criminal - der Verbrecher

cry *(v)* - weinen, schreien, rufen

crystal - das Kristal

cup - die Tasse

current - der Strom

customer - der Kunde

dad - der Vater

daddy - Papa

damn - verdammt

dance *(v)* - tanzen

danced - getanzt *(part.)*

dancing - tanzend

dark - dunkel

date - das Datum

daughter - die Tochter

day - der Tag

daily - täglich, jeden Tag

deadly - tödlich

dear - liebe

design - das Design

desk - der Schreibtisch

destroy - zerstören

develop *(v)* - entwickeln

did - tat

die *(v)* - sterben

died - starb

different - verschieden

difficult - schwer

dirty - dreckig

do *(v)* - machen

doctor - der Arzt

dog - der Hund

doll - die Puppe

door - die Tür

dorms - das Studentenwohnheim

down - nach unten

dream - der Traum

dream *(v)* - träumen

drink *(v)* - trinken

drive *(v)* - fahren

driver - der Fahrer

driving license - der Führerschein

drove - fuhr

dry *(v)* - trocknen

dry *(adj)* - trocken

DVD - die DVD

ear - das Ohr

earn *(v)* - verdienen
  I earn 10 euros per hour. - Ich verdiene 10 Euro pro Stunde.

earth - die Erde

eat *(v)* - essen

editor - der Herausgeber

education - die Ausbildung

eight - acht

eighth - achter

either of you - einer von euch

elder - älter

electric - elektrisch

eleven - elf

else - andere

e-mail - die Email

employer - der Arbeitgeber

energy - die Energie

engine - der Motor

engineer - der Ingenieur

enjoy - Spaß haben, genießen

especially - vor allem

estimate *(v)* - beurteilen

estimated - ausgewertet

etc. - usw.

evening - der Abend

every - jeder, jede, jedes

everybody - alle

everything - alles

example - das Beispiel
  for example - zum Beispiel

excuse *(v)* - sich entschuldigen

Excuse me. - Entschuldigen Sie.

experience - die Erfahrung

explain *(v)* - erklären

eye - das Auge

eyes - die Augen

face - das Gesicht

fall *(v)* - fallen

fell - fiel
  fall - der Fall

fallen - abgestürzt

falling - fallend

family - die Familie

far - weit

farm - der Bauernhof

farmer - der Bauer

fasten - anschnallen

favourite - Lieblings
  favourite film - der Lieblingsfilm

feed *(v)* - füttern

feeling - das Gefühl

female - weiblich

few - ein paar

field - das Feld

fifteen - fünfzehn

fifth - fünfter

fill up *(v)* - füllen

film - der Film

finance - die Finanzwissenschaft

find *(v)* - finden

fine - gut

finish - das Ende
  to finish - beenden

finished - fertig

fire - das Feuer

fire *(v)* - feuern

firm - die Firma

firms - die Firmen

five - fünf

flew away - flog weg

float *(v)* - treiben

floating - treiben

floor - der Boden

flow *(v)* - der Fluss

flower - die Blume

fluently - fließend

food - das Essen

foot - der Fuß
  on foot - zu Fuß

for - für

forget *(v)* - vergessen

forgot - vergass

form - das Formular

forty-four - vierundvierzig

found - gefunden

four - vier

fourth - vierte

free - frei

free time - die Freizeit, freie Zeit

freeze *(v)* - erstarren

friend - der Freund

friendly - freundlich

from - aus

from the USA - aus den USA

front - vorne

front wheels - die Vorderräder

full - voll

fun - der Spaß

funny - lustig

furniture - die Möbel

further - weiter

future - zukünftig

garden - der Garten

gas - das Gas

gave - gab

German - der Deutsche, die Deutsche

Germany - Deutschland

get *(v)* (something) - erhalten (etwas), bekommen

get *(v)* (somewhere) - ankommen

get off - aussteigen

get up - aufstehen

Get up! - Steh auf!

gift - die Begabung

girl - das Mädchen

girlfriend - die Freundin

glad - froh

glass - das Glas

go away - weggehen

go by bike, to ride a bike - Fahrrad fahren, mit dem Fahrrad fahren

gone - weg

good, well - gut

goodbye - Auf Wiedersehen

great - super, toll

green - grün

grey - grau

grey-headed - grauhaarig

guest - der Gast

gun - die Waffe

guy - der Junge

had - hatte

hair - das Haar

half - halb

hand *(v)* - geben

handcuffs - die Handschellen

happen *(v)* - passieren

happened - passiert

happiness - das Glück

happy - glücklich

hard - schwer

hat - der Hut

hate *(v)* - hassen

have *(v)* - haben

he/she/it has - er/sie/es hat

He has a book. - Er hat ein Buch.

have a lot of work - viel zu tun haben

he - er

head - der Kopf

head *(v)*, go *(v)* - gehen

health - die Gesundheit

heard - hörte

hello - hallo

help - die Hilfe

help *(v)* - helfen

helper - der Helfer

her book - ihr Buch

here (a place) - hier (Ort)

here (a direction) - hierher (Richtung)

here is - hier ist

Hey! - Hey

hi - hallo

hid - versteckte

hide *(v)* - sich verstecken

hide-and-seek - das Versteckspiel

high - hoch

him - ihm

his - sein, seine

his bed - sein Bett

hit*(v)* , beat *(v)* - schlagen

home - das Zuhause
go home - nach Hause gehen

homework - die Hausaufgaben

hope - die Hoffnung

hope *(v)* - hoffen

host - der Gastgeber

host family - die Gastfamilie

hotel - das Hotel

hotels - die Hotels

hour - die Stunde

hourly - stündlich

house - das Haus

how - wie

howling - heulend

human - der Mensch

hundred - hundert

hungry - hungrig
I am hungry. - Ich habe Hunger.

I- ich

ice-cream - das Eis

idea- die Idee

if - ob

immediately - sofort

important - wichtig

in - in

individually - einzeln

inform *(v)* - informieren, mitteilen

information - die Information, die Angabe

informed - informierte

inside - in

instead - stattdessen

instead of - anstelle von

instead of you - an deiner Stelle

interesting - interessant

Internet site - die Website

into - in

it - es

its (for neuter) - sein

jacket - die Jacke

jar - der Krug

job - die Arbeit

job agency - die Arbeitsvermittlung

join *(v)* - kommen in

journalist - der Journalist

jump *(v)* - springen

jump - der Sprung

just - einfach

kangaroo - das Känguru

kettle - der Kessel

key - der Schlüssel

keyboard - die Tastatur

killed - tötete, getötet *(part.)*

killer - der Mörder

kilometer - der Kilometer

kind, type - die Art

kindergarten - der Kindergarten

kiss *(v)* - küssen

kitchen - die Küche

kitten - das Kätzchen

knew - wusste

know *(v)* - kennen

know each other - sich kennen

lake - der See

land *(v)* - landen

language - die Sprache

laser - der Laser

last *(v)*, take *(v)* – dauern
The movie is more than three hours long.
- Der Film dauert mehr als 3 Stunden.

laugh *(v)* - lachen

leader - der Führer

learn *(v)* - lernen

learned about - kennengelernt

learning - lernen

leave *(v)* - verlassen

left - links

leg - das Bein

less - weniger

lesson - die Aufgabe, Lektion

let *(v)* - lassen

let us - lass uns

letter - der Brief

life - das Leben

life-saving trick - Rettungstrick

lift - der Aufzug

like *(v)* - gefallen

I like that. - Das gefällt mir.

like *(v)*, love *(v)* - mögen, lieben

limit - die Begrenzung

lion - der Löwe

list - die Liste

listen *(v)* - hören
  I listen to music. - Ich höre Musik.

little - klein

live *(v)* - leben, wohnen

lived - lebte

living - wohnhaft

load *(v)* - (be)laden

loader - der Verlader

long - lang

look *(v)* - schauen, betrachten

look around - sich umsehen

looked - schaute

loose *(v)* - verlieren

lot - viel

love - die Liebe

love *(v)* - lieben

loved - geliebt

machine - die Maschine

magazine - die Zeitschrift

make *(v)* - machen
  coffee-maker - die Kaffeemaschine

male - männlich

manual work - die Handarbeit

many, much - viel

map - die Karte

mattress - die Matratze

may - dürfen, können
  must not - nicht dürfen

me - mich

meanwhile - in der Zwischenzeit

medical - medizinisch

meet *(v)* - treffen, kennenlernen

member - das Mitglied

men - der Mann

mental work - die Kopfarbeit

met - getroffen, kennengelernt

metal - das Metall

meter - der Meter

method - die Methode

microphone - das Mikrofon

middle name - der zweite Name

mine - mein

minute - die Minute

Miss - Fräulein

mister, Mr. - Herr, Hr.

mobile - das Handy

mom, mother - Mama, die Mutter

moment - der Moment

Monday - Montag

money - das Geld

monkey - der Affe

monotonous - monoton

more - mehr

morning - der Morgen

mosquito - die Stechmücke

mother - die Mutter

moved - bewegte sich

much, many - viel, viele

music - die Musik

must - müssen
  I must go. - Ich muss gehen.

my - mein, meine, mein

mystery - das Rätsel

name - der Name

name *(v)* - nennen

nationality - die Nationalität

native language - die Muttersprache

nature - die Natur

nearest - nächste

nearness - die Nähe

near, nearby, next - in der Nähe

need - brauchen

neighbour - der Nachbar

never - nie

new - neu

newspaper - die Zeitung

nice - schön

night - die Nacht

nine - neun

ninth - neunter

no - nein

nobody - niemand

North America and Eurasia - Nordamerika und Eurasien

nose - die Nase

not - nicht

note - die Notiz

notebook - das Notizbuch

notebooks - die Notizbücher

nothing - nichts

now - jetzt, zurzeit, gerade

number - die Nummer

o'clock – Uhr
  It is two o'clock. - Es ist zwei Uhr.

of course - natürlich

office - das Büro

officer, policeman - der Polizist

often - oft

Oh! - Oh!

oil - das Öl

okay, well - okay, gut

on - auf

once - einmal

one - ein

one by one - einer nach dem anderen

one more - noch einen

only - nur

open *(v)* - öffnen

opened - öffnete *(past)*, geöffnet *(past p.)*

order *(v)* - befehlen

other - andere

our - unser

out of order - außer Betrieb

outdoors - draußen

over - über

own - eigen

owner - der Besitzer

pail - der Eimer

pale - blass

panic - die Panik
  to panic - in Panik versetzen

paper - das Papier

parachute - der Fallschirm

parachutist - der Fallschirmspringer

parent - die Eltern

park - der Park

parks - die Parks

part - der Teil

participant - der Teilnehmer

passed - abgelaufen

past - nach, vorbei
  at half past eight - um halb neun

patrol - die Patroiulle, die Streife

pay *(v)* - bezahlen, zahlen

paid - bezahlte, gezahlt

pay *(v)* - zahlen

pen - der Stift

pens - die Stifte

people - die Menschen

per hour - pro Stunde

person - die Person

personal - persönlich

personnel department - die Personalabteilung

pet - das Haustier

pharmacy - die Apotheke

phone handset - der Telefonhörer

phone - das Telefon

phone *(v)* - anrufen

photograph *(v)* - fotografieren

photographer - der Fotograf

phrase - der Satz

picture - das Foto

pill - die Tablette

pilot - der Pilot

pitch *(v)* - schaukeln

place *(v)* - legen

plan - der Plan

plan *(v)* - planen

planet - der Planet

plate - der Teller

play *(v)* - spielen

playing *(ger)* - spielen

please - bitte

pocket - die Tasche

pointed - richtete

Poland - Polen

police - die Polizei

poor - arm

position - die Position

possibility - die Möglichkeit

possible - möglich
  as often as possible - so oft wie möglich

pour *(v)* - schütten

prepare *(v)* - vorbereiten

press *(v)* - drücken

pretend *(v)* - vorgeben; so tun, als ob

price - der Preis

problem - das Problem

produce *(v)* - herstellen

profession - der Beruf

program - das Programm

programmer - der Programmierer

protect *(v)* - beschützen

publishing - der Verlag

pull *(v)* - ziehen

puppy - der Welpe

pursuit - die Verfolgung

push *(v)* - stoßen, ziehen

pussycat - die Miezekatze

put on - sich anziehen
dressed - angezogen

questionnaire - der Fragebogen

queue - die Schlange

quick, quickly - schnell

quietly - leise

quite - ziemlich

radar - der Radar

radio - das Radio

railway station - der Bahnhof

rain - der Regen

rang - klingelte

rat - die Ratte

read *(v)* - lesen

reading - lesend

ready - fertig

real - wirklich

really - wirklich

reason - der Grund

recommend *(v)* - empfehlen

recommendation - die Empfehlung

recommended - empfohlen

record *(v)* - aufnehmen

red - rot

refuse *(v)* - ablehnen

rehabilitate *(v)* - gesund pflegen

rehabilitation - die Genesung, Rehabilitation

remain *(v)* - bleiben

remembered - erinnerte sich

report *(v)* - berichten

reporter - der Reporter

rescue *(v)* - retten

rescue service - der Rettungsdienst

ricochet - abprallen

right - rechts

ring *(v)* - klingeln

ring - das Klingeln

road - die Straße

robber - der Dieb

robbery - der Diebstahl, der Überfall

roof - das Dach

room - das Zimmer

rooms - die Zimmer

round - rund

rub *(v)* - reiben

rubber - der Gummi

rubric - die Rubrik

rule - die Regel

run *(v)* - rennen, joggen, laufen

run away - weglaufen

running - führen

rushed - raste

sad - traurig

safe - der Tresor

said - sagte

sand - der Sand

sandwich - das Butterbrot, das Sandwich

Saturday - der Samstag

save *(v)* - retten

saw - sahen

say *(v)* - sagen

school - die Schule

sea - das Meer

seashore - die Küste

Season - die (Jahres)zeit

seat - der Sitz
take a seat - sich hinsetzen

seat belts - der Sicherheitsgurt

second - zweiter

secret - das Geheimnis

secretary - die Sekretärin

secretly - heimlich

see *(v)* - sehen

seed - das Saatgut

seldom - selten

sell *(v)* - verkaufen

sent - schickte

sergeant - der Polizeihauptmeister

serial - die Serie

seriously - ernst

servant - der Bedienstete

serve *(v)* - bedienen

set free - freisetzen

seven - sieben

seventeen (hour) - siebzehn

seventh - siebter

sex - das Geschlecht

shake *(v)* - zittern, schütteln

she - sie

sheet (of paper) - das Blatt

ship - das Schiff

shook - wackelte

shop - der Laden

shop assistant - der Verkäufer, die Verkäuferin

shopping center - das Einkaufszentrum

shops - die Läden

shore - die Küste

short - kurz

shot - schoss; angeschossen

show *(v)* - zeigen

showed - zeigte

silent, silently - leise

silly - dumm

simple - einfach

since *(temporal)* - seit
as, since *(kausal)* - da, weil

sing - singen

singer - der Sänger

single - ledig

siren - die Sirene

sister - die Schwester

sit *(v)* - setzen

sit down - sich hinsetzen

situation - die Situation

six - sechs

sixth - sechster

sixty - sechzig

skill - die Fähigkeit
sleep *(v)* - schlafen
sleeping - schlafen
slightly - leicht
slowly - langsam
sly, slyly - schlau
small - klein
smart - intelligent
smile - das Lächeln
smile *(v)* - lächeln
smiled - lächelte
snack - der Imbiss
so - deswegen
solution, answer - die Lösung
some - ein paar, einige
somebody - jemand
something - etwas
sometimes - manchmal, ab und zu
son - der Sohn
soon - bald
space - das Weltall
spaceship - das Raumschiff
spaniel - der Spaniel
Spanish - spanisch
speak *(v)* - sprechen
speech - die Rede
speed - die Geschwindigkeit
speed *(v)* - rasen
speeder - der Raser
spend *(v)* - ausgeben, verwenden
sport - der Sport
sport shop - das Sportgeschäft
sport bike - das Sportfahrrad
spread *(v)* - übergreifen
square - der Platz
stairs - die Treppe
stand *(v)* - stehen
standard - standard
star - der Stern
start *(v)* - anfangen
started (to drive) - fuhr los
status - der Stand
family status - der Familienstand
steal *(v)* - stehlen
steer *(v)* - lenken
Stefan's book - Stefans Buch
step - der Schritt
step *(v)* - treten
stepped - trat
still - noch, weiterhin
stinking - stinkend
stolen - gestohlen
stone - der Stein
stop *(v)* - anhalten
stopped - beendete
story - die Geschichte
strange - fremd
streets - die Straßen
strength - die Stärke
strong, strongly - stark
student - der Student
students - die Studenten

study *(v)* - studieren

stuffed - ausgestopft
  stuffed parachutist - Fallschirmspringerpuppe

suddenly - plötzlich

suitable - passend

supermarket - der Supermarkt

sure - klar, sicher

surprise - die Überraschung

surprise *(v)* - überraschen

surprised - überrascht, verwundert

swallow *(v)* - schlucken, hinunterschlucken

swim *(v)* - schwimmen

Swiss - Schweizer

Switzerland - die Schweiz

switched on - machte an

table - der Tisch

tables - die Tische

tail - der Schwanz

take *(v)* - nehmen

take part - teilnehmen

taken - gebracht

talk *(v)* - sich unterhalten

tanker - der Tanker

tap - der Wasserhahn

task - die Aufgabe

tasty - lecker

taxi - das Taxi

taxi driver - der Taxifahrer

tea - der Tee

teach *(v)* - beibringen

teacher - der Lehrer

team - die Mannschaft

telephone - das Telefon

telephone *(v)* - telefonieren

television - der Fernseher

tell *(v)*, say *(v)* - sagen

ten - zehn

tenth - zehnter

test - die Prüfung

test *(v)* - prüfen
  pass a test - eine Prüfung bestehen

text - der Text

textbook - das Fachbuch

than - als

Elmar is older than Linda. - Elmar ist älter als Linda.

thank *(v)* - danken

thank you, thanks - danke

that - jener, jene, jenes

that (conj) - dass
  I know that this book is interesting. - Ich weiß, dass dieses Buch interessant ist.

the same - der/die/das gleiche
  at the same time - gleichzeitig

their - ihr

then - dann

after that - danach

there - dort

these, those - diese *(pl.)*

they - sie

thief - der Dieb

thieves - die Diebe

thing - das Ding, die Sache
  this stuff - diese Dinge

think *(v)* - denken

thinking *(ger.)* - denken

third - dritter

thirty - dreißig

this - dieser, diese, dieses
this book - dieses Buch

thousand - tausend

three - drei

through - hindurch

ticket - die Fahrkarte

tiger - der Tiger

time - die Zeit

tired - müde

to be continued - Fortsetzung folgt

today - heute

together - zusammen

toilet - die Toilette

tomorrow - morgen

too, either, also - auch

took - nahm

town - die Stadt

toy - das Spielzeug

train - der Zug

train *(v)* - trainieren

trained - trainiert

translator - der Übersetzer

transport - der Transport

travel *(v)* - reisen

trick - der Trick

tried - versuchte

trousers - die Hose

truck - der Lastwagen

try *(v)* - versuchen

turn *(v)* - drehen
turn on – anmachen
turn off - ausmachen

turned - drehte

TV-set - der Fernseher

twelve - zwölf

twenty - zwanzig

twenty-five - fünfundzwanzig

twenty-one - einundzwanzig

twice - zweimal

two - zwei

unconscious - bewusstlos

under - unter

underline *(v)* - unterstreichen

understand *(v)* - verstehen

understood - verstanden

unfair - ungerecht

United States/the USA - die Vereinigten Staaten, die USA

unload *(v)* - abladen

until - bis

us - uns

use *(v)* - benutzen

usual - normal, gewöhnlich

usually - normalerweise

very - sehr

vet - der Tierarzt

videocassette - die Videokassette

video-shop - die Videothek

village - das Dorf

visited - besuchte

voice - die Stimme

wait *(v)* - warten

waited - wartete

walk *(v)* - gehen

walking - laufen

want *(v)* - wollen

wanted - wollte

war - der Krieg

warm - warm

warm up - aufwärmen

was - war

wash *(v)* - waschen, putzen

washer - die Waschmaschine

watch - die Uhr

water - das Wasser

wave - die Welle

way - der Weg

we - wir

weather - das Wetter

week - die Woche

went away - verlassen *(part.)*

were - waren

wet - nass

whale - der Wal
  killer whale - der Schwertwal

what – was
  What is this? - Was ist das?
  What table? - Welcher Tisch?

What is the matter? - Was ist los?

wheel - das Rad

when - wenn

where - wo

which - der, die, das (Konj.)

while - während

white - weiß

who - wer

whose - wessen

wide, widely - weit

will - werden

wind - der Wind

window - das Fenster

windows - die Fenster

with - mit

without – ohne
  without a word - wortlos

woman - die Frau

wonderful - wunderbar

word - das Wort, die Vokabel

words - die Wörter, die Vokabeln

worked - gearbeitet

worker - der Arbeiter

working - arbeitend

world - dic Welt

worry *(v)* - sich Sorgen machen
  Do not worry! - Mach dir keinen Kopf!

write *(v)* - schreiben

writer - der Schriftsteller

wrote - schrieb

yard - der Hof

year - das Jahr

yellow - gelb

yes - ja

yesterday - gestern

yet - noch

you - du

You - du/ihr

young - jung

your - dein

yours sincerely - hochachtungsvoll

zebra - das Zebra

zoo - der Zoo

## Starke Verben
*Strong Verbs*

| *Infinitiv* | *Präteritum* | *Perfekt (Past Participle)* |
|---|---|---|
| anfangen begin | fing an began | angefangen begun |
| ankommen arrive | kam an arrived | ist angekommen arrived |
| anrufen call up | rief an called up | angerufen called up |
| backen bake | backte baked | gebacken baked |
| befehlen command | befahl commanded | befohlen commanded |
| beginnen begin | begann began | begonnen begun |
| beißen bite | biss bit | gebissen bitten |
| bekommen get, receive | bekam got | bekommen gotten |
| bergen salvage | barg salvaged | geborgen salvaged |
| bersten burst | barst burst | geborsten burst |
| betrügen deceive | betrog deceived | betrogen deceived |
| biegen bend | bog bent | gebogen bent |
| bieten offer | bot offered | geboten offered |
| binden tie | band tied | gebunden tied |
| bitten request | bat requested | gebeten requested |
| blasen blow | blies blew | geblasen blown |
| bleiben stay | blieb stayed | ist geblieben stayed |
| bleichen bleach | blich bleached | geblichen bleached |
| braten roast | briet roasted | gebraten roasted |
| brechen break | brach broke | gebrochen broken |
| brennen burn | brannte burned | gebrannt burned |
| bringen bring | brachte brought | gebracht brought |
| denken think | dachte thought | gedacht thought |
| dreschen thresh | drosch threshed | gedroschen threshed |
| dringen force | drang forced | gedrungen forced |
| dürfen may | durfte was allowed | gedurft been allowed |
| empfangen receive | empfing received | empfangen received |

| | | |
|---|---|---|
| empfehlen recommend | empfahl recommended | empfohlen recommended |
| erfinden invent | erfand invented | erfunden invented |
| erlöschen extinguish | erlosch extinguished | erloschen extinguished |
| erschallen echo, sound | erscholl sounded | erschollen sounded |
| erschrecken scare | erschrak scared | erschrocken scared |
| essen eat | aß ate | gegessen eaten |
| fahren travel | fuhr traveled | ist gefahren traveled |
| fallen fall | fiel fell | ist gefallen fallen |
| fangen catch | fing caught | gefangen caught |
| fechten fence | focht fenced | gefochten fenced |
| finden find | fand found | gefunden found |
| fliegen fly | flog flew | ist geflogen flown |
| fliehen flee | floh fled | ist geflohen fled |
| fließen flow | floss flowed | ist geflossen flowed |
| fressen gorge | fraß gorged | gefressen gorged |
| frieren freeze | fror froze | gefroren frozen |
| frohlocken rejoice | frohlockte rejoiced | frohlockt rejoiced |
| gären ferment | gor fermented | gegoren fermented |
| gebären bear (child) | gebar bore | geboren born |
| geben give | gab gave | gegeben given |
| gedeihen flourish | gedieh flourished | ist gediehen flourished |
| gefallen be pleasing, like | gefiel liked | gefallen liked |
| gehen go | ging went | ist gegangen gone |
| gelingen succeed | gelang succeeded | ist gelungen succeeded |
| gelten be valid | galt was valid | gegolten been valid |
| genesen recover | genas recovered | genesen recovered |
| genießen enjoy | genoß enjoyed | genossen enjoyed |
| geschehen happen | geschah happened | ist geschehen happened |
| gewinnen win | gewann won | gewonnen won |
| gießen pour | goß poured | gegossen poured |

| | | |
|---|---|---|
| gleichen resemble | glich resembled | geglichen resembled |
| gleiten glide, slide | glitt glided | ist geglitten glided |
| glimmen glow | glomm glowed | ist geglommen glowed |
| graben dig | grub dug | gegraben dug |
| greifen grasp | griff grasped | gegriffen grasped |
| haben have | hatte had | gehabt had |
| halten hold | hielt held | gehalten held |
| hängen hang | hing hung/hanged | gehangen hung/hanged |
| hauen hew, hit | haute hit | gehauen hit |
| heben lift | hob lifted | gehoben lifted |
| heißen be called | hieß named | geheißen named |
| helfen help | half helped | geholfen helped |
| kennen know | kannte knew | gekannt known |
| klingen ring | klang rang | geklungen rung |
| kneifen pinch | kniff pinched | gekniffen pinched |
| kommen come | kam came | ist gekommen come |
| können can | konnte could | gekonnt could |
| kriechen crawl | kroch crawled | ist gekrochen crawled |
| laden load | lud loaded | geladen loaded |
| lassen let, allow | ließ let | gelassen let |
| laufen run | lief ran | ist gelaufen run |
| leiden suffer | litt suffered | gelitten suffered |
| leihen lend | lieh lent | geliehen lent |
| lesen read | las read | gelesen read |
| liegen lie | lag lay | gelegen lain |
| lügen lie | log lied | gelogen lied |
| mahlen grind | mahlte ground | gemahlen ground |
| meiden avoid | mied avoided | gemieden avoided |
| messen measure | maß measured | gemessen measured |
| misslingen fail | misslang failed | misslungen failed |

| | | |
|---|---|---|
| mögen like | mochte liked | gemocht liked |
| müssen must | musste had to | gemusst had to |
| nehmen take | nahm took | genommen taken |
| nennen name | nannte named | genannt named |
| pfeifen whistle | pfiff whistled | gepfiffen whistled |
| preisen praise | pries praised | gepriesen praised |
| quellen gush | quoll gushed | ist gequollen gushed |
| raten advise | riet advised | geraten advised |
| reiben rub | rieb rubbed | gerieben rubbed |
| reißen tear | riss tore | gerissen torn |
| reiten ride | ritt rode | ist geritten ridden |
| rennen run | rannte ran | ist gerannt run |
| riechen smell | roch smelled | gerochen smelled |
| ringen wring | rang wrung | gerungen wrung |
| rinnen flow | rann flowed | ist geronnen flowed |
| rufen call | rief called | gerufen called |
| salzen salt | salzte salted | gesalzen/gesalzt salted |
| saufen drink | soff drank | gesoffen drunk |
| saugen suck | sog sucked | gesogen sucked |
| schaffen create | schuf created | geschaffen created |
| scheiden depart; separate | schied separated | geschieden separated |
| scheinen shine | schien shone | geschienen shone |
| schelten scold | schalt scolded | gescholten scolded |
| schießen shoot | schoss shot | geschossen shot |
| schlafen sleep | schlief slept | geschlafen slept |
| schlagen hit | schlug hit | geschlagen hit |
| schleichen sneak | schlich sneaked | ist geschlichen sneaked |
| schleifen polish | schliff polished | geschliffen polished |
| schließen close, lock | schloss closed | geschlossen closed |
| schlingen gulp (down) | schlang gulped | geschlungen gulped |

| | | |
|---|---|---|
| schmeißen fling, toss | schmiss flung | geschmissen flung |
| schmelzen melt | schmolz melted | geschmolzen melted |
| schneiden cut | schnitt cut | geschnitten cut |
| schrecken scare | schrak/schreckte scared | geschreckt/geschrocken scared |
| schreiben write | schrieb wrote | geschrieben written |
| schreien scream | schrie screamed | geschrien screamed |
| schreiten step | schritt stepped | ist geschritten stepped |
| schweigen be silent | schwieg was silent | geschwiegen been silent |
| schwellen swell, rise | schwoll swelled | ist geschwollen swollen |
| schwimmen swim | schwamm swam | ist geschwommen swum |
| schwinden dwindle | schwand dwindled | ist geschwunden dwindled |
| schwingen swing | schwang swung | geschwungen swung |
| schwören swear | schwur/schwor swore | geschworen sworn |
| sehen see | sah saw | gesehen seen |
| sein be | war was | ist gewesen been |
| senden send, transmit | sandte sent | gesandt sent |
| sieden boil | sott/siedete boiled | gesotten boiled |
| singen sing | sang sang | gesungen sung |
| sinken sink | sank sank | ist gesunken sunk |
| sitzen sit | saß sat | gesessen sat |
| sollen should, ought to | sollte should | gesollt should |
| spalten split | spaltete split | gespalten/gespaltet split |
| speien spew | spie spewed | gespien spewed |
| spinnen spin | spann spun | gesponnen spun |
| sprechen speak | sprach spoke | gesprochen spoken |
| sprießen sprout | spross sprouted | gesprossen sprouted |
| springen jump | sprang jumped | ist gesprungen jumped |
| stechen stab, sting | stach stung | gestochen stung |
| stehen stand | stand stood | gestanden stood |
| stehlen steal | stahl stole | gestohlen stolen |

| steigen climb | stieg climbed | ist gestiegen climbed |
|---|---|---|
| sterben die | starb died | ist gestorben died |
| stieben fly about | stob flew about | ist gestoben flown about |
| stinken stink | stank stank | gestunken stunk |
| stoßen push, bump | stieß pushed | gestoßen pushed |
| streichen strike, paint | strich struck | gestrichen struck |
| streiten argue | stritt argued | gestritten argued |
| tragen carry, wear | trug wore | getragen worn |
| treffen meet | traf met | getroffen met |
| treiben move, drive | trieb drove | getrieben driven |
| triefen drip | triefte/troff dripped | getrieft dripped |
| trinken drink | trank drank | getrunken drunk |
| trügen be deceptive | trog was deceptive | getrogen been deceptive |
| tun do | tat did | getan done |
| überwinden overcome | überwand overcame | überwunden overcome |
| verderben spoil | verdarb spoiled | verdorben spoiled |
| verdrießen annoy | verdross annoyed | verdrossen annoyed |
| vergessen forget | vergaß forgot | vergessen forgotten |
| verlieren lose | verlor lost | verloren lost |
| verschleißen wear (out) | verschliss wore (out) | verschlissen worn (out) |
| verzeihen forgive | verzieh forgave | verziehen forgiven |
| wachsen grow | wuchs grew | ist gewachsen grown |
| waschen wash | wusch washed | gewaschen washed |
| weben weave | wob/webte wove | gewoben/gewebt woven |
| weichen yield | wich yielded | ist gewichen yielded |
| weisen indicate | wies indicated | gewiesen indicated |
| wenden turn | wandte turned | gewandt turned |
| werben recruit | warb recruited | geworben recruited |
| werden become | wurde became | ist geworden become |
| werfen throw | warf threw | geworfen thrown |

| | | |
|---|---|---|
| wiegen weigh | wog/wiegte weighed | gewogen/gewiegt weighed |
| winden twist | wand twisted | gewunden twisted |
| wissen know | wusste knew | gewusst known |
| wollen want to | wollte wanted to | gewollt wanted to |
| wringen wring | wrang wrung | gewrungen wrung |
| zeihen accuse | zieh accused | geziehen accused |
| ziehen pull | zog pulled | gezogen pulled |
| zwingen compel | zwang compelled | gezwungen compelled |

## List of the most common words

| Tage der Woche | Days of the week |
|---|---|
| Der Sonntag | Sunday |
| Der Montag | Monday |
| Der Dienstag | Tuesday |
| Der Mittwoch | Wednesday |
| Der Donnerstag | Thursday |
| Der Freitag | Friday |
| Der Samstag | Saturday |
| Die Woche | week |
| Der Tag | day |
| Die Nacht | night |
| heute | today |
| gestern | yesterday |
| morgen | tomorrow |
| Der Morgen | morning |
| Der Abend | evening |
| **Die Monate** | **Months** |
| Der Januar | January |
| Der Februar | February |
| Der März | March |
| Der April | April |
| Der Mai | May |
| Der Juni | June |
| Der Juli | July |
| Der August | August |
| Der September | September |
| Der Oktober | October |
| Der November | November |
| Der Dezember | December |

| Die Jahreszeiten | Seasons of the year |
|---|---|
| Der Winter | winter |
| Der Frühling | spring |
| Der Sommer | summer |
| Der Herbst | autumn |
| **Die Familie** | **Family** |
| Die Tante | aunt |
| Der Bruder | brother |
| Die Kinder | children |
| Der Papa | dad |
| Die Tochter | daughter |
| Die Familie | family |
| Der Vater | father |
| Die Enkelin | granddaughter |
| Der Großvater | grandfather |
| Die Oma | grandmother |
| Die Großeltern | grandparents |
| Der Enkel | grandson |
| Der Urgroßvater | great-grandfather |
| Die Urgroßmutter | great-grandmother |
| Die Mutter | mother |
| Der Neffe | nephew |
| Die Nichte | niece |
| Die Eltern | parents |
| Die Schwester | sister |
| Der Sohn | son |
| Der Onkel | uncle |

| Aussehen und Qualitäten | Appearance and qualities |
|---|---|
| aktiv | active |
| kahl | bald |
| Der Charakter | character |
| klug | clever |
| rücksichtsvoll | considerate |
| kreativ | creative |
| grausam | cruel |
| lockig | curly |
| energetisch | energetic |
| fett | fat |
| großzügig | generous |
| gierig | greedy |
| behaart | hairy |
| gut aussehend | handsome |
| freundlich | kind |
| verheiratet | married |
| alt | old |
| rundlich | plump |
| höflich | polite |
| arm | poor |
| ziemlich | pretty |
| reich | rich |
| unhöflich | rude |
| kurz | short |
| einzig | single |
| dünn | skinny |
| schlank | slim |
| gerade | straight |
| stark | strong |
| blöd | stupid |
| taktvoll | tactful |
| talentiert | talented |
| hoch | tall |
| dünn | thin |
| hässlich | ugly |
| unfreundlich | unkind |
| schwach | weak |
| jung | young |

| Emotionen | Emotions |
|---|---|
| gelangweilt | bored |
| zuversichtlich | confident |
| zufrieden | content |
| neugierig | curious |
| begeistert | ecstatic |
| Die Emotion | emotion |
| aufgeregt | excited |
| doof | goofy |
| glücklich | happy |
| hoffend | hoping |
| hungrig | hungry |
| einsam | lonely |
| spitzbübisch | mischievous |
| nervös | nervous |
| beleidigt | offended |
| traurig | sad |
| erschrocken | scared |
| schockiert | shocked |
| schläfrig | sleepy |
| überrascht | surprised |

| | |
|---|---|
| durstig | thirsty |
| müde | tired |
| **Kleider** | **Clothes** |
| Der Anorak | anorak |
| Der Gürtel | belt |
| Die Bluse | blouse |
| Der Stiefel | boots |
| Das Armband | bracelet |
| Die Kappe | cap |
| Die Strickjacke | cardigan |
| Die Kleider | clothes |
| Der Mantel | coat |
| Das Kleid | dress |
| Der Ohrring | earring |
| Der Pelzmantel | fur coat |
| Die Brille | glasses |
| Der Handschuh | glove |
| Der Hut | hat |
| Die Jacke | jacket |
| Die Jeans | jeans |
| Das Trikot | jersey |
| Die Halskette | necklace |
| Das Nachthemd | nightie |
| Der Pyjama | pyjamas |
| Die Regenjacke | raincoat |
| Der Ring | ring |
| Die Sandalen | sandals |
| Der Schal | scarf |
| Das Hemd | shirt |
| Die Schuhe | shoes |
| Die kurze Hose | shorts |
| Der Rock | skirt |
| Die Hausschuhe | slippers |
| Die Turnschuhe | sneakers |
| Die Socken | socks |
| Die Strümpfe | stockings |
| Der Anzug | suit |
| Das Sweatshirt | sweater |
| Der Badeanzug | swimsuit |
| Die Krawatte | tie |
| Die Strumpfhose | tights |
| Der Trainingsanzug | tracksuit |
| Die Hose | trousers |
| Das T-Shirt | T-shirt |
| Der Regenschirm | umbrella |
| Die Hose | pants |
| Die Uhr | watch |
| **Haus und Möbel** | **House and furniture** |
| Der Wecker | alarm clock |
| Die Wohnung | apartment |
| Der Balkon | balcony |
| Das Badezimmer | bathroom |
| Das Bett | bed |
| Das Schlafzimmer | bedroom |
| Die Tagesdecke | bedspread |
| Die Bank | bench |
| Die Decke | blanket |
| Das Bücherregal | bookcase |
| Der Teppich | carpet |
| Die Schatulle | casket |

| | | | |
|---|---|---|---|
| Der Sessel | chair | Die Dusche | shower |
| Der Wandschrank | closet | Das Sofa | sofa |
| Der Schrank | cupboard | Die Treppe | stairs |
| Der Vorhang | curtain | Der Schemel | stool |
| Der Schreibtisch | desk | Die Tabelle | table |
| Das Esszimmer | dining room | Die Toilette | toilet |
| Die Tür | door | nach oben | upstairs |
| Die Türklingel | doorbell | Das Fenster | window |
| unten | downstairs | **Die Küche** | **Kitchen** |
| Die Möbel | furniture | Der Brenner | burner |
| Die Garage | garage | Der Küchenschrank | cabinet |
| Der Flur | hall | Der Kanister | canister |
| Der Korridor | hallway | Der Sessel | chair |
| Das Haus | house | Das Kochbuch | cookbook |
| Das Innere | interior | Der Geschirrspüler | dishwasher |
| Die Küche | kitchen | Der Wasserhahn | faucet |
| Die Lampe | lamp | Der Gefrierschrank | freezer |
| Das Wohnzimmer | living room | Die Küche | kitchen |
| Der Briefkasten | mailbox | Das Geschirr | kitchenware |
| Die Matratze | mattress | Die Mikrowelle | microwave |
| Der Spiegel | mirror | Der Ofen | oven |
| Der Nachttisch | nightstand | Der Kühlschrank | refrigerator |
| Das Bild | picture | Das Waschbecken | sink |
| Das Kissen | pillow | Der Schwamm | sponge |
| Der Kissenbezug | pillowcase | Der Herd | stove |
| Das Dach | roof | Die Tabelle | table |
| Das Zimmer | room | Der Toaster | toaster |
| Der Safe | safe | Das Handtuch | towel |
| Das Blatt | sheet | **Das Geschirr** | **Tableware** |
| Das Regal | shelf | Die Flasche | bottle |

| | | | |
|---|---|---|---|
| Die Schüssel | bowl | Der Kaviar | caviar |
| Die Kaffeetasse | coffeepot | Der Käse | cheese |
| Die Tasse | cup | Das Hähnchen | chicken |
| Die Gabel | fork | Die Schokolade | chocolate |
| Die Bratpfanne | frying pan | Der Cocktail | cocktail |
| Das Glas | glass | Der Kakao | cocoa |
| Der Krug | jug | Der Kaffee | coffee |
| Der Kessel | kettle | Das Plätzchen | cookie |
| Das Messer | knife | Das Croissant | croissant |
| Der Deckel | lid | Das Kotelett | cutlet |
| Der Becher | mug | Das Ei | egg |
| Die Serviette | napkin | Der Fisch | fish |
| Die Pfanne | pan | Das Mehl | flour |
| Der Pfefferstreuer | pepper shaker | Das Lebensmittel | food |
| Der Teller | plate | gebraten | fried |
| Der Salzstreuer | salt shaker | Die Frucht | fruit |
| Der Kochtopf | saucepan | Der Schinken | ham |
| Der Löffel | spoon | Das Eis | ice cream |
| Die Zuckerschüssel | sugar bowl | Die Marmelade | jam |
| Das Geschirr | tableware | Das Gelee | jelly |
| Die Teekanne | teapot | Der Saft | juice |
| **Essen** | **Food** | Der Ketchup | ketchup |
| gebacken | baked | Die Makkaroni | macaroni |
| Die Bohne | bean | Die Mayonnaise | mayonnaise |
| Das Rindfleisch | beef | Das Fleisch | meat |
| bitter | bitter | Die Milch | milk |
| Das Brot | bread | Der Pfannkuchen | pancake |
| Die Butter | butter | Die Pasta | pasta |
| Der Kuchen | cake | Der Pfeffer | pepper |
| Die Süßigkeiten | candy | Der Kuchen | pie |

| | | | |
|---|---|---|---|
| Die Pizza | pizza | Die Nieren | kidneys |
| Das Schweinefleisch | pork | Das Geflügel | poultry |
| Der Haferbrei | porridge | Das Hähnchen | chicken |
| Die Kartoffel | potato | Der Truthahn | turkey |
| Der Reis | rice | Die Ente | duck |
| Der Salat | salad | Die Gans | goose |
| Das Salz | salt | Der Fisch | fish |
| gesalzen | salted | Der Kabeljau | cod |
| Das Sandwich | sandwich | Die Forelle | trout |
| Die Soße | sauce | Der Lachs | salmon |
| Die Wurst | sausage | Der Seehecht | hake |
| Die Suppe | soup | Die Scholle | plaice |
| sauer | sour | Die Makrele | mackerel |
| würzen | spice | Die Sardine | sardine |
| Das Steak | steak | Der Hering | herring |
| Der Zucker | sugar | Die Meeresfrüchte | seafood |
| süß | sweet | Die Garnele | prawn |
| Der Tee | tea | Die Garnele | shrimp |
| Das Gemüse | vegetables | Die Muschel | mussel |
| **Fleisch und Fisch** | **Meat and fish** | Die Auster | oyster |
| Das Fleisch | meat | Der Hummer | lobster |
| Das Rindfleisch | beef | Der Tintenfisch | squid |
| Das Lamm | lamb | Die Krabbe | crab |
| Das Hammelfleisch | mutton | **Die Frucht** | **Fruit** |
| Das Schweinefleisch | pork | Der Apfel | apple |
| Das Kalbfleisch | veal | Die Aprikose | apricot |
| Das Wild | venison | Die Banane | banana |
| Der Speck | bacon | Die Frucht | fruit |
| Der Schinken | ham | Die Traube | grape |
| Die Leber | liver | Die Grapefruit | grapefruit |

| | |
|---|---|
| Die Kiwi | kiwi |
| Die Zitrone | lemon |
| Die Limette | lime |
| Die Mango | mango |
| Die Melone | melon |
| Der Pfirsich | peach |
| Die Birne | pear |
| Die Ananas | pineapple |
| Die Pflaume | plum |
| **Das Gemüse** | **Vegetables** |
| Die Bohnen | beans |
| Die Zuckerrüben | beet |
| Der Kohl | cabbage |
| Die Karotte | carrot |
| Der Sellerie | celery |
| Die Gurke | cucumber |
| Der Dill | dill |
| Die Aubergine | eggplant |
| Der Knoblauch | garlic |
| Die Zwiebel | onion |
| Die Petersilie | parsley |
| Die Erbse | pea |
| Der Pfeffer | pepper |
| Die Kartoffel | potato |
| Der Kürbis | pumpkin |
| Der Rettich | radish |
| Die Tomate | tomato |
| Das Gemüse | vegetable |
| **Die Getränke** | **Beverages** |
| Alkohol | alcohol |
| alkoholisches | alcoholic |
| Getränk | beverage |
| Das Bier | beer |
| Das Getränk | beverage |
| Der Cocktail | cocktail |
| Der Kakao | cocoa |
| Der Kaffee | coffee |
| Das Getränk | drink |
| Der Fruchtsaft | fruit juice |
| Der Eistee | iced tea |
| Der Saft | juice |
| Die Limonade | lemonade |
| Die Milch | milk |
| Der Milchshake | milkshake |
| Der Orangensaft | orange juice |
| Das alkoholfreie Getränk | soft drink |
| Der Tee | tea |
| Der Tomatensaft | tomato juice |
| Der Gemüsesaft | vegetable juice |
| Das Wasser | water |
| Der Wein | wine |
| **Das Kochen** | **Cooking** |
| hinzufügen | add |
| backen | bake |
| schlagen | beat |
| kochen | boil |
| hacken | chop |
| kochen | cook |
| kochend | cooking |
| braten | fry |
| reiben | grate |

| | |
|---|---|
| grillen | grill |
| schmelzen | melt |
| zerkleinern | mince |
| mischen | mix |
| schälen | peel |
| gießen | pour |
| braten | roast |
| sieben | sift |
| kochen | simmer |
| schneiden | slice |
| rühren | stir |
| waschen | wash |
| wiegen | weigh |
| verquirlen | whisk |
| **Der Haushalt** | **Housekeeping** |
| Die Luft | air |
| bleichen | bleach |
| Der Besen | broom |
| Der Eimer | bucket |
| Das Reinigungsmittel | cleanser |
| Die Wäscheklammer | clothespin |
| Der Schmutz | dirt |
| Der Staub | dust |
| Die Schaufel | dustpan |
| leer | empty |
| Der Müll | garbage |
| Die Haushaltung | housekeeping |
| Das Bügeleisen | iron |
| Das Bügelbrett | ironing board |
| Die Wäsche | laundry |
| Das Waschmittel | laundry detergent |
| Der Mopp | mop |
| Der Lappen | rag |
| Der Schwamm | sponge |
| fegen | sweep |
| Der Mülleimer | trash can |
| Der Staubsauger | vacuum cleaner |
| wischen | wipe |
| **Die Körperpflege** | **Body care** |
| Die Pflege | care |
| Das Eau de Cologne | cologne |
| Der Kamm | comb |
| Die Zahnseide | dental floss |
| Das Deodorant | deodorant |
| Der Ventilator | fan |
| Das Erfrischungsmittel | freshener |
| Die Haarnadel | hairpin |
| Der Korb | hamper |
| Die Hygiene | hygiene |
| Der Lippenstift | lipstick |
| Die Wimperntusche | mascara |
| Der Spiegel | mirror |
| Das Mundwasser | mouthwash |
| Die Nagelpolitur | nail polish |
| Das Parfüm | perfume |
| Der Rasierer | razor |
| Die Waage | scale |
| Die Schere | scissors |
| Das Shampoo | shampoo |
| Der Rasierschaum | shaving cream |

| | | | |
|---|---|---|---|
| Die Dusche | shower | Das Wetter | weather |
| Das Waschbecken | sink | Der Wind | wind |
| Die Seife | soap | windig | windy |
| Der Schwamm | sponge | **Der Transport** | **Transport** |
| Die Toilette | toilet | Das Flugzeug | airplane |
| Die Zahnbürste | toothbrush | Der Krankenwagen | ambulance |
| Die Zahnpasta | toothpaste | Das Fahrrad | bicycle |
| Das Handtuch | towel | Das Boot | boat |
| Die Pinzette | tweezers | Der Bus | bus |
| **Das Wetter** | **Weather** | Das Auto | car |
| Die Brise | breeze | Der Hubschrauber | helicopter |
| hell | bright | Das Motorrad | motorcycle |
| frostig | chilly | Das Polizeiauto | police car |
| bewölkt | cloudy | Die Straße | road |
| kalt | cold | Das Segelboot | sailboat |
| kühl | cool | Der Roller | scooter |
| Der Nebel | fog | Das Schiff | ship |
| neblig | foggy | Die Straße | street |
| eisig | frosty | Die Ampel | traffic light |
| Der Hagel | hail | Der Zug | train |
| Die Hitze | heat | Die Tram | tram |
| heiß | hot | Der Transport | transport |
| Der Blitz | lightning | Der LKW | truck |
| Der Nebel | mist | Der Van | van |
| Der Regen | rain | **Die Stadt** | **City** |
| regnerisch | rainy | Die Gasse | alley |
| Der Regenschauer | shower | Der Bereich | area |
| Der Schnee | snow | Die Allee | avenue |
| sonnig | sunny | Die Bäckerei | bakery |
| Die Temperatur | temperature | Die Bank | bank |

| | |
|---|---|
| Die Bar | bar |
| Die Badeanstalt | baths |
| Die Bank | bench |
| Die Buchhandlung | bookstore |
| Die Brücke | bridge |
| Das Gebäude | building |
| Die Bushaltestelle | bus stop |
| Das Café | cafe |
| Der Parkplatz | car park |
| Die Kirche | church |
| Das Kino | cinema |
| Der Zirkus | circus |
| Die Stadt | city |
| Das Café | coffee shop |
| Die Ecke | corner |
| Die Kreuzung | crossing |
| Die Fußgängerbrücke | crosswalk |
| Die Zahnarztpraxis | dentist's |
| Das Kaufhaus | department store |
| Der Arzt | doctor's |
| Die Drogerie | drugstore |
| Die Feuerwehr | fire station |
| Das Blumengeschäft | flower shop |
| Das Blumenbeet | flower-bed |
| Der Brunnen | fountain |
| Die Galerie | gallery |
| Die Tankstelle | gas station |
| Das Tor | gate |
| Der Friseur | hair salon |
| Das Krankenhaus | hospital |

| | |
|---|---|
| Das Hotel | hotel |
| Die Straßenkreuzung | intersection |
| Die Bibliothek | library |
| Die Karte | map |
| Der Markt | market |
| Das Monument | monument |
| Das Kino | movie theater |
| Das Museum | museum |
| Der Nachtclub | nightclub |
| Der Palast | palace |
| Der Park | park |
| Der Parkplatz | parking lot |
| Das Pflaster | pavement |
| Der Zebrastreifen | pedestrian crossing |
| Die Apotheke | pharmacy |
| Die Bildergalerie | picture gallery |
| Die Polizei | police |
| Das Schwimmbad | pool |
| Die Post | post office |
| Das Restaurant | restaurant |
| Die Straße | road |
| Das Straßenschild | road sign |
| Die Schule | school |
| Der Sitz | seat |
| Das Geschäft | shop |
| Der Bürgersteig | sidewalk |
| Der Wolkenkratzer | skyscraper |
| Der Platz | square |
| Das Stadion | stadium |
| Der Stall | stall |

| | |
|---|---|
| Die Statue | statue |
| Das Geschäft | store |
| Die Straße | street |
| Die Straßenkarte | street map |
| Der Vorort | suburb |
| Die U-Bahn | subway |
| Der Supermarkt | supermarket |
| Das Schwimmbad | swimming pool |
| Der Taxistand | taxi-rank |
| Das Theater | theatre |
| Die Stadt | town |
| Der Stadtplan | town plan |
| Der Stadtplatz | town square |
| Die Ampeln | traffic lights |
| Der Bahnhof | train station |
| Die Untergrundbahn | underground |
| Die Unterführung | underpass |
| Die Universität | university |
| Der Zoo | zoo |
| **Die Schule** | **School** |
| Der Rucksack | backpack |
| Die Glocke | bell |
| Die Biologie | biology |
| Die Tafel | blackboard |
| Die Unterbrechung | break |
| Der Taschenrechner | calculator |
| Der Sessel | chair |
| Die Kreide | chalk |
| Die Chemie | chemistry |
| Die Klemme | clamp |
| Das Klassenzimmer | classroom |
| Der Clip | clip |
| Das Klemmbrett | clipboard |
| Die Uhr | clock |
| Die Korrekturflüssigkeit | correction fluid |
| Der Lehrplan | curriculum |
| Der Schreibtisch | desk |
| Die Zeichnung | drawing |
| Die Bildung | education |
| Der Radiergummi | eraser |
| Die Prüfung | exam |
| Die Untersuchung | examination |
| Die Datei | file |
| Die Erdkunde | geography |
| Der Globus | globe |
| kleben | glue |
| Der Schulleiter | headmaster |
| Der Textmarker | highlighter |
| Die Geschichte | history |
| Der Urlaub | holiday |
| Die Lektion | lesson |
| Das Schließfach | locker |
| Die Karte | map |
| Das Kennzeichen | mark |
| Der Marker | marker |
| Die Mathematik | mathematics |
| Die Musik | music |
| Das Notizbuch | notebook |
| Der Notizblock | notepad |
| Der Bürobedarf | office supplies |

| | |
|---|---|
| Das Papier | paper |
| Der Stift | pen |
| Der Bleistift | pencil |
| Das Mäppchen | pencil case |
| Die Physik | physics |
| der Locher | puncher |
| Der Schüler | pupil |
| Die Reißzwecke | pushpin |
| Das Lineal | ruler |
| Die Schule | school |
| Die Schere | scissors |
| Der Tesafilm | scotch tape |
| Das Semester | semester |
| Der Anspitzer | sharpener |
| Der Hefter | stapler |
| Die Heftklammern | staples |
| Die Schreibwaren | stationery |
| Der Aufkleber | sticker |
| Der Schüler | student |
| Das Band | tape |
| Der Lehrer | teacher |
| Der Test | test |
| Das Lehrbuch | textbook |
| Der Zeitplan | timetable |
| **Die Berufe** | **Professions** |
| Der Buchhalter | accountant |
| Der Schauspieler | actor |
| Der Administrator | administrator |
| Der Architekt | architect |
| Der Künstler | artist |
| Der Athlet | athlete |
| Der Herrenfriseur | barber |
| Der Barkeeper | barman |
| Der Leibwächter | bodyguard |
| Der Erbauer | builder |
| Der Kassierer | cashier |
| Der Reiniger | cleaner |
| Der Trainer | coach |
| Der Komponist | composer |
| Der Berater | consultant |
| Der Koch | cook |
| Der Kurier | courier |
| Der Zahnarzt | dentist |
| Der Designer | designer |
| Der Arzt | doctor |
| Der Fahrer | driver |
| Der Ökonom | economist |
| Der Elektriker | electrician |
| Der Ingenieur | engineer |
| Der Financier | financier |
| Der FeuerwehrmannDer | fireman |
| Der Führer | guide |
| Der Friseur | hairdresser |
| Der Dolmetscher | interpreter |
| Der Journalist | journalist |
| Der Anwalt | lawyer |
| Der Bibliothekar | librarian |
| Manager | manager |
| Der Soldat | military (man) |
| Der Musiker | musician |

| | |
|---|---|
| Die Krankenschwester | nurse |
| Der Fotograf | photographer |
| Der Klempner | plumber |
| Der Polizist | policeman |
| Der Politiker | politician |
| Der Briefträger | postman |
| Der Priester | priest |
| Der Beruf | profession |
| Der Programmierer | programmer |
| Der Wissenschaftler | scientist |
| Die Sekretärin | secretary |
| Der Verkäufer | shop assistant |
| Der Sänger | singer |
| Der Stylist | stylist |
| Der Taxifahrer | taxi driver |
| Der Lehrer | teacher |
| Der Tierarzt | vet |
| Die Bedienung | waiter |
| Der Schriftsteller | writer |
| **Die Aktionen** | **Actions** |
| biegen | bend |
| tragen | carry |
| fangen | catch |
| kriechen | crawl |
| tauchen | dive |
| ziehen | drag |
| schlagen | hit |
| halten | hold |
| hüpfen | hop |
| springen | jump |
| treten | kick |
| lehnen | lean |
| aufheben | lift |
| marschieren | march |
| ziehen | pull |
| drücken | push |
| stellen | put |
| laufen | run |
| sitzen | sit |
| überspringen | skip |
| schlagen | slap |
| hocken | squat |
| strecken | stretch |
| werfen | throw |
| auf Zehenspitzen gehen | tiptoe |
| gehen | walk |
| **Die Musik** | **Music** |
| Die musikalische Begleitung | accompaniment |
| Das Akkordeon | accordion |
| Das Album | album |
| Der Dudelsack | bagpipe |
| Die Balalaika | balalaika |
| Das Ballett | ballet |
| Das Band | band |
| Der Bass | bass |
| Das Fagott | bassoon |
| Der Taktstock | baton |
| Der Bogen | bow |
| Die Blechbläser | brass instruments |

| | |
|---|---|
| Das Cello | cello |
| Die Kammermusik | chamber music |
| Die Klarinette | clarinet |
| Die klassische Musik | classical music |
| komponieren | compose |
| Der Komponist | composer |
| Das Konzert | concert |
| Der Dirigent | conductor |
| Das Becken | cymbals |
| Die Trommel | drum |
| Die Trommelstöcke | drum sticks |
| Die Flöte | flute |
| Der Konzertflügel | grand piano |
| Die Gitarre | guitar |
| Die Harfe | harp |
| Das Horn | horn |
| Die Instrumentalmusik | instrumental music |
| Der Lautsprecher | loudspeaker |
| Das Mikrofon | microphone |
| Die Musikinstrumente | musical instruments |
| Der Musiker | musician |
| Die Oboe | oboe |
| Die Oper | opera |
| Die Operette | operetta |
| Das Orchester | orchestra |
| Die Orgel | organ |
| Das Schlagzeug | percussion |
| Das Klavier | piano |
| Die Aufführung | recital |
| Das Saxophon | saxophone |
| Die Single | single |
| Der Solist | soloist |
| Das Lied | song |
| Der Klang | sound |
| Die Streichinstrumente | string instruments |
| Die Symphonie | symphony |
| Der Synthesizer | synthesizer |
| transkribieren | transcribe |
| Die Posaune | trombone |
| Die Trompete | trumpet |
| Die Tuba | tuba |
| Das Video (Clip) | video (clip) |
| Die Viola | viola |
| Die Geige | violin |
| Der Virtuose | virtuoso |
| Die Blasinstrumente | wind instruments |

| **Der Sport** | **Sports** |
|---|---|
| Das Aerobic | aerobics |
| die Leichtathletik | athletics |
| Das Basketballspiel | basketball |
| Das Bowling | bowling |
| Das Boxen | boxing |
| Der Kanusport | canoeing |
| Das Radfahren | cycling |
| Das Tanzen | dancing |
| Das Tauchen | diving |
| Das Fußballspiel | football |
| Das Golf | golf |
| Die Gymnastik | gymnastics |

| | |
|---|---|
| Das Eishockey | hockey |
| Das Jogging | jogging |
| Das Judo | judo |
| Das Karate | karate |
| Das Fallschirmspringen | parachuting |
| Das Tischtennis | ping-pong |
| Das Rennen | racing |
| Das Segeln | sailing |
| Das Schießen | shooting |
| Das Skateboarding | skateboarding |
| Das Skaten | skating |
| Das Skifahren | skiing |
| Das Schlittenfahren | sledding |
| Das Schwimmen | swimming |
| Das Fußballspiel | soccer |
| Das Tennis | tennis |
| Das Volleyballspiel | volleyball |
| Das Gewichtheben | weightlifting |
| Das Ringen | wrestling |
| Das Segeln | yachting |
| **Der Körper** | **Body** |
| Der Knöchel | ankle |
| Der Arm | arm |
| Der Rücken | back |
| kahl | bald |
| Der Bart | beard |
| Der Körper | body |
| Das Gesäß | bottom |
| Die Waden | calf (calves) |
| Die Wange | cheek |
| Die Brust | chest |
| Das Kinn | chin |
| Der Ellbogen | elbow |
| Das Auge (die Augen) | eye(s) |
| Die Augenbraue | eyebrow |
| Die Wimper | eyelash |
| Das Augenlid | eyelid |
| Das Gesicht | face |
| Der Finger | finger |
| Der Fingernagel | fingernail |
| Der Fuß ( die Füße) | foot (feet) |
| Die Stirn | forehead |
| Die Brille | glasses |
| Das Haar | hair |
| behaart | hairy |
| Die Hand | hand |
| Der Kopf | head |
| Die Hacke | heel |
| Der Zeigefinger | index finger |
| Das Knie | knee |
| Das Bein | leg |
| Die Lippe(n) | lip(s) |
| Der kleine Finger | little finger |
| Der Mann | man |
| Der Mittelfinger | middle finger |
| Der Schnurrbart | moustache |
| Der Mund | mouth |
| Der Hals | neck |
| Die Nase | nose |
| Die Handinnenfläche | palm |

| | |
|---|---|
| Die Pupille | pupil |
| Der Ringfinger | ring finger |
| Das Schienbein | shin |
| Die Schulter | shoulder |
| Der Bauch | stomach |
| Die Sonnenbrille | sunglasses |
| Der Schenkel | thigh |
| Der Daumen | thumb |
| Die Zehe | toe |
| Der Zehennagel | toenail |
| Die Zunge | tongue |
| Der Zahn (die Zähne) | tooth (teeth) |
| Die Taille | waist |
| Die Frau | woman |
| **Die Natur** | **Nature** |
| Der Strand | beach |
| Die Schlucht | canyon |
| Die Küste | coast |
| Die Wüste | desert |
| Das Feld | field |
| Der Wald | forest |
| Der Gletscher | glacier |
| Der Hügel | hill |
| Die Höhle | hollow |
| Die Insel | island |
| Der Dschungel | jungle |
| Die See | lake |
| Der Berg | mountain |
| Die Natur | nature |
| Der Ozean | ocean |
| Die Ebene | plain |
| Der Teich | pond |
| Der Fluss | river |
| Der Felsen | rock |
| Das Meer | sea |
| **Das Haustier** | **Pet** |
| Die Katze | cat |
| Der Hund | dog |
| Das Meerschweinchen | guinea pig |
| Der Hamster | hamster |
| Das Pferd | horse |
| Das Kätzchen | kitten |
| Das Haustier | pet |
| Das Schwein | pig |
| Das Ferkel | piglet |
| Der Welpe | puppy |
| Der Hase | rabbit |
| **Die Tiere** | **Animals** |
| Das Tier | animal |
| Die Fledermaus | bat |
| Der Bär | bear |
| Der Biber | beaver |
| Der Bison | bison |
| Das Kamel | camel |
| Der Schimpanse | chimpanzee |
| Der Hirsch | deer |
| Der Esel | donkey |
| Der Elefant | elephant |
| Der Fuchs | fox |
| Die Giraffe | giraffe |

| | |
|---|---|
| Der Gorilla | gorilla |
| Das Nilpferd | hippopotamus |
| Das Pferd | horse |
| Die Hyäne | hyena |
| Das Känguru | kangaroo |
| Der Koala | koala |
| Der Leopard | leopard |
| Der Löwe | lion |
| Das Lama | llama |
| Der Affe | monkey |
| Der Elch | moose |
| Die Maus | mouse |
| Der Pandabär | panda |
| Das Schwein | pig |
| Der Hase | rabbit |
| Die Ratte | rat |
| Das Nashorn | rhinoceros |
| Der Skunk | skunk |
| Das Eichhörnchen | squirrel |
| Der Tiger | tiger |
| Der Wolf | wolf |
| Das Zebra | zebra |
| **Die Vögel** | **Birds** |
| Der Vogel | bird |
| Der Kanarienvogel | canary |
| Das Hühnchen | chicken |
| Der Kranich | crane |
| Die Krähe | crow |
| Der Kuckuck | cuckoo |
| Die Ente | duck |
| Der Adler | eagle |
| Der Flamingo | flamingo |
| Die Gans | goose |
| Der Falke | hawk |
| Der Kolibri | hummingbird |
| Der Vogel Strauß | ostrich |
| Die Eule | owl |
| Der Papagei | parrot |
| Der Pfau | peacock |
| Der Pelikan | pelican |
| Der Pinguin | penguin |
| Der Fasan | pheasant |
| Die Taube | pigeon |
| Die Möwe | seagull |
| Der Spatz | sparrow |
| Der Storch | stork |
| Die Schwalbe | swallow |
| Der Schwan | swan |
| Der Specht | woodpecker |
| **Die Blumen** | **Flowers** |
| Der Strauß | bouquet |
| Die Kamelie | camellia |
| Die Nelke | carnation |
| Der Krokus | crocus |
| Die Narzisse | daffodil |
| Die Dahlie | dahlia |
| Das Gänseblümchen | daisy |
| Der Löwenzahn | dandelion |
| Die Blume | flower |
| Die Gladiole | gladiolus |

| | |
|---|---|
| Die Iris | iris |
| Das Lavendel | lavender |
| Die Lilie | lily |
| Der Lotus | lotus |
| Die Narzisse | narcissus |
| Die Orchidee | orchid |
| Die Pfingstrose | peony |
| Der Mohn | poppy |
| Die Rose | rose |
| Das Schneeglöckchen | snowdrop |
| Die Sonnenblume | sunflower |
| Die Tulpe | tulip |
| Das Veilchen | violet |
| **Die Bäume** | **Trees** |
| Die Akazie | bark |
| Die Buche | beech |
| Die Birke | birch |
| Der Ast | branch |
| Die Kastanie | chestnut |
| Der Kegel | cone |
| Die Tanne | fir |
| Der Wald | forest |
| Das Blatt | leaf |
| Die Linde | linden |
| Der Ahorn | maple |
| Die Eiche | oak |
| Die Palme | palm |
| Die Kiefer | pine |
| Die Pappel | poplar |
| Die Wurzel | root |
| Der Baum | tree |
| Der Baumstamm | trunk |
| Die Weide | willow |
| **Das Meer** | **Sea** |
| Der Alligator | alligator |
| Der Cachalot | cachalot |
| Die Koralle | coral |
| Die Krabbe | crab |
| Der Flusskrebs | crayfish |
| Das Krokodil | crocodile |
| Der Delfin | dolphin |
| Der Fisch | fish |
| Der Frosch | frog |
| Die Qualle | jellyfish |
| Der Hummer | lobster |
| Das Weichtier | mollusc |
| Der Ozean | ocean |
| Der Tintenfisch | octopus |
| Der Otter | otter |
| Das Meer | sea |
| Die Seeschlange | sea snake |
| Der Seehund | seal |
| Der Hai | shark |
| Die Meeresfrüchte | shellfish |
| Die Garnele | shrimp |
| Die Schnecke | snail |
| Der Seestern | starfish |
| Der Schwertfisch | swordfish |
| Die Schildkröte | tortoise |
| Die Schildkröte | turtle |

| | |
|---|---|
| Das Walross | walrus |
| Der Wal | whale |
| **Die Farben** | **Colors** |
| gelb | Yellow |
| grün | green |
| blau | blue |
| braun | brown |
| weiß | white |
| rot | red |
| orange | orange |
| rosa | pink |
| grau | gray |
| schwarz | black |
| **Die Größe** | **Size** |
| Die Größe | size |
| klein | small |
| groß | big |
| mittel | medium |
| klein | little |
| groß | large |
| enorm | huge |
| lang | long |
| kurz | short |
| breit | wide |
| eng | narrow |
| hoch | high |
| groß | tall |
| niedrig | low |
| tief | deep |
| flach | shallow |
| dick | thick |
| dünn | thin |
| weit | far |
| in der Nähe von | near |
| **Die Materialien** | **Materials** |
| Der Ziegel | brick |
| Der Karton | cardboard |
| Der Lehm | clay |
| Das Tuch | cloth |
| Der Beton | concrete |
| Das Glas | glass |
| Das Leder | leather |
| Das Material | material |
| Das Metall | metal |
| Das Papier | paper |
| Der Kunststoff | plastic |
| Das Gummi | rubber |
| Der Stein | stone |
| Das Holz | wood |
| Der Stoff | fabric |
| **Der Flughafen** | **Airport** |
| Das Flugzeug | (air)plane |
| Der Flughafen | airport |
| Der Gang | aisle |
| Die Armlehne | armrest |
| Der Rucksack | backpack |
| Das Gepäck | baggage |
| Das Einsteigen | boarding |
| Die Kabine | cabin |
| Das Fortfahren | carry-on |

| | |
|---|---|
| Der Cockpit | cockpit |
| Der Zoll | customs |
| Die Verzögerung | delay |
| Das Reiseziel | destination |
| Der Notfall | emergency |
| Der Flug | flight |
| Der Rumpf | fuselage |
| Das Gate | gate |
| Die Landung | landing |
| Die Toilette | lavatory |
| Die Rettungsweste | life vest |
| Die Flüssigkeit | liquid |
| Der Passagier | passenger |
| Der Reisepass | passport |
| Die Startbahn | runway |
| Der Zeitplan | schedule |
| Der Sitz | seat |
| Der Sicherheitsbeamte | security, guard |
| Der Koffer | suitcase |
| Das Heck | tail |
| Das Abheben | takeoff |
| Der Terminal | terminal |
| Die Fahrkarte | ticket |
| Der Wagen | trolley |
| Das Fahrwerk | undercarriage |
| Das Visum | visa |
| Das Fenster | window |
| Der Flügel | wing |
| **Die Erdkunde** | **Geography** |
| Der Bereich | area |
| Die Hauptstadt | capital |
| Die Stadt | city |
| Das Land | country |
| Der Kreis | district |
| Die Region | region |
| Das Bundesland | state |
| Die Stadt | town |
| Das Dorf | village |
| Das Kap | cape |
| Das Kliff | cliff |
| Der Gletscher | glacier |
| Der Hügel | hill |
| Der Berg | mountain |
| Die Bergkette / Bergkette - | mountain chain - |
| Der Pass | pass |
| Die Spitze | peak |
| Die Ebene | plain |
| Das Plateau | plateau |
| Der Gipfel | summit |
| Das Tal | valley |
| Der Vulkan | volcano |
| Die Wüste | desert |
| Der Äquator | equator |
| Der Wald | forest |
| Das Hochland | highlands |
| Der Dschungel | jungle |
| Das Tiefland | lowlands |
| Die Oase | oasis |
| Der Sumpf | swamp |
| Die Tropen | tropics |

| | |
|---|---|
| Die Tundra | tundra |
| Der Kanal | canal |
| Die See | lake |
| Der Ozean | ocean |
| Die Meeresströmung | ocean current |
| Der Pool / Teich | pool / pond |
| Der Fluss | river |
| Das Meer | sea |
| Die Quelle | spring |
| Der Strom | stream |

| **Das Verbrechen** | **Crimes** |
|---|---|
| Die Brandstiftung | arson |
| Der Angriff | assault |
| Die Bigamie | bigamy |
| Die Erpressung | blackmail |
| Die Bestechung | bribery |
| Der Einbruch | burglary |
| Der Kindesmissbrauch | child abuse |
| Die Verschwörung | conspiracy |
| Die Spionage | espionage |
| Die Fälschung | forgery |
| Der Betrug | fraud |
| Der Völkermord | genocide |
| Die Entführung | hijacking |
| Der Mord | homicide |
| Die Entführung | kidnapping |
| Der Totschlag | manslaughter |
| Der Überfall | mugging |
| Der Mord | murder |
| Der Meineid | perjury |
| Die Vergewaltigung | rape |
| Das Randalieren | riot |
| Der Raub | robbery |
| Der Ladendiebstahl | shoplifting |
| Die Verleumdung | slander |
| Der Schmuggel | smuggling |
| Der Verrat | treason |
| Das unerlaubte Betreten | trespassing |

| **Nummern** | **Numbers** |
|---|---|
| eins | one |
| zwei | two |
| drei | three |
| vier | four |
| fünf | five |
| sechs | six |
| Sieben | seven |
| acht | eight |
| neun | nine |
| zehn | ten |
| elf | eleven |
| zwölf | twelve |
| dreizehn | thirteen |
| vierzehn | fourteen |
| fünfzehn | fifteen |
| sechzehn | sixteen |
| siebzehn | seventeen |
| achtzehn | eighteen |
| neunzehn | nineteen |
| zwanzig | twenty |
| einundzwanzig | twenty-one |

| | |
|---|---|
| zweiundzwanzig | twenty-two |
| dreißig | thirty |
| vierzig | forty |
| fünfzig | fifty |
| sechzig | sixty |
| siebzig | seventy |
| achtzig | eighty |
| neunzig | ninety |
| einhundert | one hundred |
| einhundertundeins ... | one hundred and one ... |
| zweihundert | two hundred |
| eintausend | one thousand |
| eine Million | one million |
| **Ordnungszahlen** | **Ordinal numbers** |
| erste | first |
| zweite | second |
| dritte | third |
| vierte | fourth |
| fünfte | fifth |
| sechste | sixth |
| siebte | seventh |
| achte | eighth |
| neunte | ninth |
| zehnte | tenth |
| elfte | eleventh |
| zwölfte | twelfth |
| dreizehnte | thirteenth |
| vierzehnte | fourteenth |
| fünfzehnte | fifteenth |
| sechzehnte | sixteenth |
| siebzehnte | seventeenth |
| achtzehnte | eighteenth |
| neunzehnte | nineteenth |
| zwanzigste | twentieth |
| einundzwanzigste | twenty-first |
| zweiundzwanzigste | twenty-second |
| dreiundzwanzigste | twenty-third |
| vierundzwanzigste | twenty-fourth |
| fünfundzwanzigste | twenty-fifth |
| sechsundzwanzigste | twenty-sixth |
| siebenundzwanzigste | twenty-seventh |
| achtundzwanzigste | twenty-eighth |
| neunundzwanzigste | twenty-ninth |
| dreißigste | thirtieth |
| vierzigste | fortieth |
| fünfzigste | fiftieth |
| sechzigste | sixtieth |
| siebzigste | seventieth |
| achtzigste | eightieth |
| neunzigste | ninetieth |
| hundertste | hundredth |
| tausendste | thousandth |
| millionste | millionth |

## Recommended reading

### First German Reader for Beginners (Volume 1)

**Bilingual for Speakers of English**

***Beginner Elementary (A1 A2)***

The book consists of Elementary and Pre-intermediate courses with parallel German-English texts. The author maintains learners' motivation by funny stories about real life situations such as meeting people, studying, job searches, working etc. The ALARM Method (Approved Learning Automatic Remembering Method) utilize natural human ability to remember words used in texts repeatedly and systematically. The author had to compose each sentence using only words explained in previous chapters. The second and the following chapters of the Elementary course have only about thirty new words each. The audio tracks are available inclusive on www.lppbooks.com/German

### First German Reader (Volume 2)

**Bilingual for Speakers of English**

***Elementary (A2)***

This book is Volume 2 of First German Reader for Beginners. There are simple and funny German texts for easy reading. The book consists of Elementary course with parallel German-English texts. The author maintains learners' motivation with funny stories about real life situations such as meeting people, studying, job searches, working etc. The ALARM method utilize natural human ability to remember words used in texts repeatedly and systematically. The audio tracks and samples are available inclusive on www.lppbooks.com/German

### First German Reader (Volume 3)

**Bilingual for Speakers of English**

***Elementary (A2)***

This book is Volume 3 of First German Reader for Beginners. There are simple and funny German texts for easy reading. The book consists of Elementary course with parallel German-English texts. The author maintains learners' motivation with funny stories about real life situations such as meeting people, studying, job searches, working etc. The ALARM method utilize natural human ability to remember words used in texts repeatedly and systematically. The audio tracks and samples are available inclusive on www.lppbooks.com/German

## Second German Reader
### Bilingual for Speakers of English
### *Elementary Pre-Intermediate (A2 B1)*

A private detective is following the girl he is in love with. A former air force pilot, he is discovering some sides in the human nature he can't deal with. This book makes use of the ALARM Method to efficiently teach its reader German words, sentences and dialogues. The audio tracks and samples are available inclusive on www.lppbooks.com/German

## First German Reader for Beginners
### Bilingual for Children and Parents
### *Beginner (A1)*

The book contains a beginner's course for children with parallel German-English translation. There are a few pictures and the first simple sentences in the first chapter. More pictures and vocabulary are added in the second and following chapters. They build up little stories, guiding a learner gently into the English language. The method ALARM utilize natural human ability to remember words used in texts repeatedly and systematically. The audio tracks and samples are available inclusive on www.lppbooks.com/German

## First German Reader for Students
### Bilingual for Speakers of English
### *Beginner Elementary (A1 A2)*

German language learners can learn vocabulary and grammar usage with First German Reader for Students easily and fast. Each chapter is filled with words that are organized by topic, then used in a story in German. Questions and answers rephrase information and text is repeated in English to aid comprehension. The quick and easy-to-use format organizes many of life's situations from knowing your way around the house, studying at university, or getting a job. First German Reader for Students makes use of the ALARM Method to efficiently teach its reader German words, sentences and dialogues. The audio tracks and samples are available inclusive on www.lppbooks.com/German

## First German Reader for Cooking

### Bilingual for Speakers of English

### *Beginner Elementary (A1 A2)*

When learning a language, familiarity in the subject helps connect one language to another. The First German Reader for Cooking provides the words and phrases in both English and German. Twenty-five chapters are divided into themes and topics related to cooking and food. Recipe directions along with easy questions and answers demonstrate the usage of these words and phrases. Supplementary resources include the German/English and English/German dictionaries. It might make you hungry or it might help German language learners like you improve their understanding in a familiar setting of the kitchen. The audio tracks and samples are available inclusive on www.lppbooks.com/German

## First German Reader for Business

### Bilingual for Speakers of English

### *Beginner Elementary (A1 A2)*

The German you learn in high school or college does not always include the vocabulary you need in a professional environment. The First German Reader for Business is a resource that guides conversational bilinguals with the German vocabulary, phrases, and questions that are relevant to many situations in the workplace. With 25 chapters on topics from the office to software and supplementary resources including the German/English and English/German dictionaries, it is the book to help the businessperson take their German language knowledge to the professional level. The audio tracks and samples are available inclusive on www.lppbooks.com/German

## First German Medical Reader for Health Professions and Nursing Bilingual for Speakers of English

### Bilingual for Speakers of English

### Beginner Elementary (A1 A2)

First German Medical Reader will give you the words and phrases necessary for helping patients making appointments, informing them of their diagnosis, and their treatment options. Medical specialties range from ENT to dentistry. The ALARM method utilize natural human ability to remember words used in texts repeatedly and systematically. The author composed each sentence using only words explained in previous chapters. Supplementary resources include the German/English and English/German dictionaries, audio tracks, the 1300 important German words. Use this book to take your German knowledge to the health professional's level. The audio tracks are available inclusive on www.lppbooks.com/German/FGMR/

## First German Reader for the Family

### Bilingual for Speakers of English

### Beginner Elementary (A1 A2)

How do you ask in a clear and precise way about relatives of your friends? How do you answer questions about your family and other beloved ones? Ask and answer questions about situations at home, on your way to school or university, at work, in hospital etc. The book makes use of the ALARM Method to efficiently teach its reader German words, sentences and dialogues. Through this method, a person will be able to enhance his or her ability to remember the words that has been incorporated into consequent sentences. The audio tracks and samples are available inclusive on www.lppbooks.com/German

## Thomas's Fears and Hopes

### Short Stories in Plain Spoken German

### Bilingual for speakers of English

### Pre-intermediate Level

Thomas had returned home to Georgia for his father's funeral. He became informed that he would receive the entire estate as he was the only child. Then a few events happened that scared him. The audio tracks are available inclusive on www.lppbooks.com/German/SSPSG/

## First German Reader for Tourists

### Bilingual for Speakers of English

### Beginner (A1)

If you would like to travel and learn German at A1 level, this book is the best choice. Unlike a phrasebook, it is composed with the thought of systematic learning approach. The book makes use of the ALARM Method to efficiently teach its reader German words, sentences and dialogues. Through this method, a person will be able to enhance his or her ability to remember the words that has been incorporated into consequent sentences. The audio tracks and samples are available inclusive on www.lppbooks.com/German

## Learn German Language Through Dialogue
### Bilingual for Speakers of English
### Beginner Elementary (A1 A2)

The textbook gives you a lot of examples on how questions in German should be formed. It is easy to see the difference between German and English using parallel translation. Common questions and answers used in everyday situations are explained simply enough even for beginners. Some sayings and jokes make it engaging despite four cases that make German a little difficult for some students. The audio tracks and samples are available inclusive on www.lppbooks.com/German

## Die Abenteuer von Benny & Ollie in gefährlichen Situationen

Tips for discussing child safety and what you can do to help your child. Tips for parents to help their children stay safe and what your child can do. Outside and at home. This bilingual book contains German-English parallel translation.

## Fremde Wasser
### Intermediate German Reader
### Parallel translation for speakers of English

Being a co-founder of a two-men business has it's pros and cons. However the cold waters of self-employment do not fit everyone. The audio tracks are available inclusive on www.lppbooks.com/German/BSE

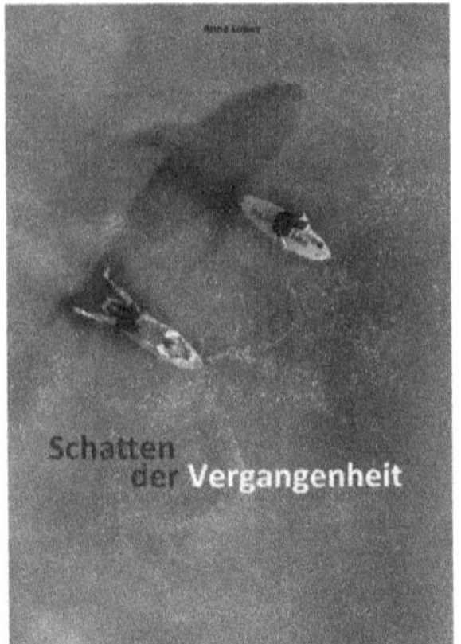


## Schatten der Vergangenheit
### Intermediate level
### Bilingual for Speakers of English

Forensic science was one of Damien Morin's passions. However, the first real crime that he investigated led him to his own past. The audio tracks are available inclusive on www.audiolego.com/German/Lopez/En

**Wer verlor das Geld? Who lost the money?**
**First German Reader for Beginner and Elementary Level**
**Bilingual with German-English Translation**

The first part of the book explains with examples of basic sentence structure of German language. The German and English texts are located parallel for easier understanding. Each chapter contains patterns of basic sentence structure according to two or three grammar topics. The second part of the book, which is also composed of simple sentences, represents a detective story. The ALARM method utilize natural human ability to remember words used in texts repeatedly and systematically. The audio tracks are available inclusive on www.lppbooks.com/German/WLM/

www.ingramcontent.com/pod-product-compliance
Lightning Source LLC
LaVergne TN
LVHW081317110826
845149LV00006B/1534

* 9 7 8 8 3 6 6 0 1 1 2 6 7 *